LAW WITHOUT LAWYERS, JUSTICE WITHOUT COURTS

This book is dedicated

in honour of the memory of my late grandmother, Madam Tan Sok
who taught me about Humanity and Love

to my parents, Mr Goh Ming Foo and Madam Tong Siow
who have given me Love

to my husband, Chamkaur, and our daughter, Mindy
who inspire Love

Law Without Lawyers, Justice Without Courts
On traditional Chinese mediation

GOH Bee Chen
Associate Dean (Undergraduate Studies) & Associate Professor of Law, Bond University, Australia

Ashgate

Published by
Ashgate Publishing Limited
Gower House
Croft Road
Aldershot
Hampshire GU11 3HR
England

Ashgate Publishing Company
131 Main Street
Burlington, VT 05401-5600 USA

Ashgate website: http://www.ashgate.com

British Library Cataloguing in Publication Data
GOH, Bee Chen
    Law without lawyers, justice without courts : on
    traditional Chinese mediation
    1.Mediation - China 2.Mediation - China - History
    I.Title
    303.6'9'0951

Library of Congress Control Number: 2002100902

ISBN 1 84014 744 X

Printed and bound by Athenaeum Press, Ltd.,
Gateshead, Tyne & Wear.

Contents

Preface

Let householders avoid litigation, for once go to law and there is nothing but trouble.

To enter a court of law is to enter a tiger's mouth.
- Chinese proverbs.

This book bears a legal anthropological flavour. Ethnologically, the Chinese have been renowned for their non-litigiousness. The above Chinese proverbs serve as truisms. As such, the main aim of this book is to analyze the Chinese non-litigious outlook and trace their cultural preference for the informal dispute resolution process, primarily in the form of mediation. The inquiry involves examining the Chinese legal tradition by delving into its ancient origins and by examining the Law in the social context. It has been found that mediation has worked well with the Chinese because its practice agrees with the Chinese cultural tradition. Such a convergence of cultural theory with practice perpetuates to this day. For instance, if we take even a cursory look at the current commercial legislation of the People's Republic of China, we are bound to notice an ever-present emphasis on the requirement and thus, the first recourse to mediate disputes.

This book also presents a cross-cultural theme. The term 'mediation' has differing cultural connotations in the Western and Chinese contexts. I use 'mediation' in this book in the sense of a means of settling disputes with third party assistance using informal procedures which result in non-binding decisions except for communal pressures necessitating voluntary compliance. Western literature on Alternative Dispute Resolution (popularized as 'ADR') appears reluctant to approach the subject of mediation in the same 'loose' way. In the West, there is a constant striving for analytic purity, resulting in attempts at precise definitions of 'mediation', 'mediation-arbitration', 'conciliation', and so on. These purist strands have been branded 'classical' or 'orthodox'. At best, a pedantic Western mediator may look at my use of 'mediation' here as resembling 'conciliation'. I make no apologies. I think, instead, it is more important to appreciate that *there are* varying cultural undertones in the practices of mediation East and West, rather than try to disengage oneself from that reality through definitional compensation. As such, I regard it as important that I include a chapter on cross-cultural observations in mediation.

This piece of work has spanned over nearly two decades, beginning with my initial undergraduate research and culminating in my current specialization in ADR. Certainly, I have witnessed tremendous changes over this period, not only in relation to traditional Chinese mediation, but also the rapid emergence of the use of mediation in Western countries. I can still recall attending an international conference on this theme in Kuala Lumpur in 1984 and my American counterparts, including a judge, were fascinated by my research findings into the rural Chinese Malaysian practice of traditional dispute settlement. The American judge from California, in fact, took a copy of my research piece with him so that he could learn more about traditional Chinese preference for informal dispute resolution. When I came to Bond in 1991, mediation was emerging in Australia as a buzz-word. In the last decade, the Bond Law School's Dispute Resolution Centre has helped to entrench the discipline and the practice of ADR in Australia. Mediation has definitely come a long way and is here to stay.

The term 'Chinese' as used in this book is primarily an ethnological reference. As such, the assertions are applicable to the global Chinese communities, and where references are confined to rural Chinese, or Chinese Malaysians, they will be so stated.

The structure of the book is organized as follows:

- Chapter 1 offers cross-cultural insights on the nature of mediation in the East and in the West.
- Chapter 2 traces the Chinese legal tradition as being chiefly responsible for the characteristic Chinese non-litigiousness.
- In the absence of a reliance on the formal law, Chapter 3 touches upon the prevailing traditional norms, customary precepts and social sanctions as being relevant in the Chinese way of life by providing the effective social control mechanisms.
- Chapter 4 examines the reasons why the Chinese have abhorred the formal courts and why mediation has prevailed.
- In Chapter 5, the perpetuation of non-litigiousness and promotion of mediation is demonstrated through a look at rural Chinese Malaysian communities.
- Finally, some concluding remarks are presented in Chapter 6.

GOH Bee Chen
Bond Law School, Australia

March 2002

Acknowledgements

'...thanks, and thanks, and ever thanks.'
Sebastian: Act III, Scene II, in William Shakespeare,
Twelfth Night.

My labour of love has not been without challenges. But, I remain always grateful to the many people who have, whether they are aware of it or not, helped this work materialize, including my students at the Bond Law School who have undertaken courses in 'Chinese Negotiation' and 'Dispute Resolution in Asia' with me.

My first thanks go to Mr Haji Sulaiman Abdullah, now a legal practitioner in Malaysia. This initial research choice of examining the non-litigious character of the Chinese was his brainchild. I also wish to express my heartfelt thanks to Professor R H Hickling: this book is 'better late than never'. I could not hope to have been able to spend the time on my research and writing if not for the indulgence of an extremely understanding faculty and work environment. This is especially so given that I became a 'full-time' mother, and multi-tasking and juggling were the order of the day. I, therefore, wish to record my appreciation to the Bond Law School. I also wish to acknowledge the superb research facilities and conducive academic environment of the Institute of Advanced Legal Studies in London where I was fortunate enough to spend a research semester as a Visiting Scholar in 1998.

As usual, my natal family is my backbone. More relevantly, my family members, in every extended Chinese sense, have contributed to my empirical research. My thanks to them are eternal. I always tell my husband, Chamkaur, that 'behind every aspiring woman is a starving husband' and to him, I owe everything... To our daughter, Mindy, this is a book for her by a mother who needed to extricate herself from playtime with her as a necessary sacrifice, but who hopes that she will continue with the task of keeping the peace by perpetuating her mediation heritage.

GOH Bee Chen.

1 On Mediation: Sino-Western Insights

We may share the same bed but we dream different dreams.[1]

Introduction

Disputes are natural and inevitable occurrences in every society where social contact tends to produce power struggles, tension and friction.[2] However, this is not to say that disputes are a bad thing: far from it. As Boulle rightly observes, conflicts may yield 'positive benefits'.[3] These benefits include 'opportunities for introspection, review and renewal, for the restoration of personal and business relationships, and for establishing new arrangements for the future'.[4]

Critically, how a society adopts or utilizes the means to resolve disputes will depend on its available resources, and, as I will argue here, on its ingrained cultural inclinations and philosophic leanings. In short, there are present cultural imperatives in guiding disputing behaviour.[5] In the words of Merry:

> Disputing, however, is cultural behaviour, informed by participants' moral views about how to fight, the meaning participants attach to going to court, social practices that indicate when and how to escalate disputes to a public forum, and participants' notions of rights and entitlement. Parties to a dispute operate within systems of meaning; they seek ways of doing things that seem right, normal or fair, often acting out of habit or moral conviction. The normative framework shapes the way people conceptualize problems, the ways they pursue them, and the kinds of solutions they look for.[6]

In our modern times, the popularity of mediation as a means of alternative dispute resolution can hardly be understated. The rapid growth in the use of mediation in Western countries such as the United States of America and Australia in the last two decades has been simply astounding. 'Australia in the early 1990s is witness to a new wave of enthusiasm for alternative dispute resolution (ADR)'.[7] However, as observed by Palmer:

> '... it is clear that we cannot find in Western and many other formal legal systems the same kind and degree of emphasis that in the PRC is officially attached to the role of extra-judicial mediation... in the resolution of civil disputes and the handling of minor criminal offenses'.[8]

Thus, when we look at both Chinese and Western mediations, the former has been in existence since ancient times while the latter is a comparatively recent phenomenon.[9] The entrenched prevalence of mediation in Eastern countries such as the People's Republic of China and Japan may be attributed to culture which allows mediation to evolve naturally and imperceptibly, as well as in a deeply meaningful way. Culture here is used in a wide sense to encompass the entirety of the belief systems, the habits, the behaviour patterns, and the unconscious tendencies of particular groups.[10] For instance, the cultural tradition of the Chinese, with reference to disputes and their settlement, will include their philosophic attachments, and the involvement of the formal and informal institutions.

The traditional Chinese context as seen here is very similar to the one demonstrated by the indigenous Australian society. As asserted by Astor and Chinkin:

> It should not be forgotten that Aboriginal people have resolved disputes without recourse to litigation, or anything resembling it, since time immemorial. At the time of the British invasion of Australia Aboriginal people had a well developed system of law based on a kinship system which prescribed rights and obligations over the whole spectrum of activities. If obligations under the law were ignored or flouted there were various ways of dealing with transgressors, including exclusion from the community, arrangements for compensation, more rigorous forms of initiation or training, and public ridicule or shaming.[11]

Boulle refers to such contexts as 'communally-based systems of managing conflict'.[12] Their characteristic features are a closely-knit social system with high-ranking elders acting as mediators who perform the binary role of conflict solver and public peacekeeper, who wield personal authority and enforce social sanctions.[13] However, because cultural influences are variable, indeterminate, and uncertain, the virtues of traditional mediation are not without criticisms by interested onlookers, with references to such traditional practices conjuring 'myths and fictions'.[14] I am, nevertheless, unconvinced by such observations. Traditional styles of mediation, as exemplified by the Chinese, remain a significant source of social peacekeeping. It is naturally evolving, intuitive, and easily identifiable by the participants operating in the same cultural matrix. Because cultures can evolve over time, there may be a shift of cultural norms resulting in a change in participant behaviour and expectations. For instance, traditional Chinese mediation appears not to flourish as well in urban Chinese communities because fundamentally, the cultural norms are different: economic ties replace personal ties, and commercial values rank higher than social values. In such circumstances, it is necessary that the actors resort to modern practices, whatever they may be, and traditional norms are seen to give way.

As I see it, culture as a shaper and regulator in dispute resolution represents an unseen and unacknowledged force.[15] Indeed, as Hall puts it, it is the continuation of the 'cultural unconscious'[16] which we constantly experience, and as Hall further asserts, such an experience is more particularly evident in Western culture. Culture does undoubtedly play a significant role in the perception, conception, management and settlement of disputes in every society.[17] For example, in a comparative study between the Americans and the Japanese on conflict strategies, the following was observed:

> [The Americans] prefer to defend themselves actively, employing or developing the rationale for positions they have taken. When pushed they may resort to still more aggressive forms that utilize humor, sarcasm, or denunciation. Among Japanese, the reactions are more varied, but defenses tend to be more passive, permit withdrawal, and allow greater concealment.[18]

Generally speaking, Western culture has always pursued democratic rights, individual justice and for this purpose, has used the communicative tools of open debate and confrontation to achieve its goals. In contrast, Eastern culture has always cherished political stability, social harmony and towards these ends, has adopted subtle persuasion and conflict avoidance techniques in communication. In the East, for instance, the suppression of disputes is a common phenomenon. In this connection, Lubman and Wajnowski record, with regard to mainland Chinese commercial dispute resolution, that whenever foreigners deem that there exist Sino-foreign commercial disputes, from the Chinese counterparts, the 'common reactions have been disbelief, shock, surprise or... denial that a dispute exists at all'.[19] Similarly, as remarked by Gudykunst, 'Chinese, for example, would advise an executive to meet with an insulter and the target of the insult separately so that conflict between the two can be avoided.'[20]

In Western culture, individualistic ideals promote the establishment of legal institutions as private guardians. The formal law is viewed with supremacy and power.[21] Consequently, litigation has been much encouraged as the prime and primary method in the settling of disputes. Litigation also concords with the Western individualistic tendency for confrontational behaviour.[22] This is still the dominant trend despite the vast growth of mediation in the West which has encouraged informal dispute settlement via mediation. By way of contrast, the Chinese habits tend to promote mediation or conciliation as the main or primary method of dispute resolution. In fact, Chinese society is generally regarded as litigation-averse. The Chinese cultural tradition chiefly accounts for such an attitude, as will be demonstrated in later Chapters. However, this is not to say that mediation does not enjoy a personal/cultural flavour with the West. The argument here is more one of degree rather than substance.

Comparative Approaches To Mediation

Mediation is a common term used in both East and West. However, I would venture to suggest that we are, in fact, referring to a similar activity with differing connotations when we approach the subject of mediation from the different Eastern and Western cultural angles.[23] These different connotations are the consequences of culture. As pointed out by Clarke:

It is clear that the set of institutions and practices going generally under the name of 'mediation' (*tiaojie*) in China is of great importance in the field of dispute resolution. It is equally clear, however, that what is called mediation in China is very different from what is called mediation in the ADR literature, to the point where it would be seriously misleading simply to use the English word without further explanation.[24]

Similarly, Moser observes the following with regard to the Chinese use of mediation:

> … in actual practice the Chinese concept of mediation, or *tiaojie*, is highly malleable. It may be characterised, on the one hand, as a "flexible and blended procedure of concessions, arrangements [and] compromises"… while at other times it may take on some of the coercive aspects of adjudication.[25]

In the following sections, I shall discuss salient features which support the notion that the nature of mediation in the West and in the East operates on the basis of their respective cultural orientations. This observation is so made given that traditional Chinese mediation comes across as intuitive and informal and reflects collectivistic ideals, whereas modern Western mediation is recognized as being more formal and structured and is reflective of individualistic principles.

Western Individualism And Chinese Collectivism

By and large, the traits implicit in Western individualism and Chinese collectivism account for the greatest cultural divergence to mediation as a means of settling disputes.[26] This knowledge may surprise a few, especially those untrained in cross-cultural issues or considerations. However, one must not pretend that all members of a particular culture behave in a homogenous fashion. What may be true is the observation that there are fundamental traits which may appear consistently so as to form a coherent and systematic pattern of behaviour which, in turn, makes it plausible for certain generalizations to be made.[27] In my analysis, the cultural variant pertaining to Western individualism and Chinese collectivism, at the outset, colours a spectrum of matters associated with a dispute. The way a disputant may perceive a range of matters has a great deal to do with his or her own dominant cultural background.[28]

At this point, it is also important to clarify that rarely is a person an extreme individualist or an extreme collectivist. We are usually cultural concocts. Having said that, our concoction carries dominant flavours. Each one of us can be *pre-dominantly* an individualist or *pre-dominantly* a collectivist.[29] It is this pre-dominance which greatly influences our perceptual abilities. And, our perception, by and large, determines our framework regarding how a dispute arises and how it can be contained or resolved.[30] A culture much influenced by the precept of harmony (as is the case with the collectivists) will tend to avoid disputes to the extent that minor disagreements are ignored, in the hope that they disappear of their own accord.[31] This is the classic case of conflict avoidance. Conversely, a culture much geared towards the notions of rights and justice (as is the case with the individualists) will tend to be confrontational, even with minor things, so much so that there is always a risk of an escalation of conflicts. In the latter culture, it is deemed unnatural and unhealthy to suppress disputes. In the West, to 'speak one's mind' represents a popular social injunction.[32]

It has become almost trite to describe individualism as essentially founded upon self-centred or egocentric values.[33] Such values orientate an individualist's pursuit of happiness primarily on self-realization and self-expression and self-creativity.[34] She or he regards herself or himself as the focal point of existence. All else matters not; at least not in the way that it is not self-serving. An individualistic person is inclined to put personal welfare above others, and to find meaning in activities which generate the same kind of self-importance or self-righteousness. As Weldon and Jehn posit thus, 'in an individualist society, people value autonomy, assertiveness, competition, and individual achievement'.[35] Such individualistic ideals would tend to mould the individualistic person's perception and management of disputes, in almost unconscious ways. For, culture is, after all, the 'silent language'.[36]

Western individualism tends to promote freedom of action, which, in turn, emphasizes competitiveness and acquisitiveness. This is particularly evident in materialistic matters. In Auerbach's words, 'Individualism means freedom - above all, the freedom to compete, acquire, possess, and bequeath'.[37] Such values undoubtedly inculcate, nurture and produce a predominantly assertive and confrontational nature in individualistic persons. In the pursuit of individualistic ideals, most notably individual rights and justice, such a culture naturally looks to the law as an institution for the protection of private rights and preservation of civil liberties.[38] The Rule of Law is an oft-quoted norm. There is no denying the fact that legal institutions are viewed as paramount guardians of individual rights and promoters of personal justice. The Rule of Law, in the West, is thus commonly perceived as the foundation of a normative social order. As such, in the event of disputes, litigation is seen as the natural way of resolving disputes. Litigation, by extension, is a facet of confrontational culture. As Auerbach puts it, 'as rights are asserted, combat is encouraged; as the rule of law binds society, legal contentiousness increases social fragmentation'.[39] In short, the rights of the individual override the social, or group goals. Such a feature remains a predominant phenomenon in individualism.

In contrast, in the case of the Chinese, collectivism is the norm. 'In a collectivist society, social relationships and group welfare dominate individual needs and desires'.[40] Collectivism, therefore, emphasizes upon group or communal goals.[41] These goals are founded upon the collective welfare of all, with the submergence of individual interests.[42] Rather, a more precise way of observing this phenomenon is to assert that the individual submits to the objectives of the group as a means of preserving or advancing his or her own interests. As Hsu observes, the problem for the Chinese 'has always been how to make the individual live according to accepted customs and rules of conduct, not how to enable him to rise above them'.[43]

In Chinese collectivism, the group is thus seen as the protector and regulator of individual behaviour and expected outcomes.[44] Such a group acts as the central functionary which can be the family, society, community or country to which the person claims membership.[45] Collectivists also tend to differentiate between in-groups and out-groups,[46] and it is the former which play an important socio-political role by exerting a strong sphere of influence in respect of its members.[47] The major in-groups are one's family, work colleagues, or educational institutions.[48]

Triandis succinctly posits the individualism-collectivism dichotomy thus:

> In individualist cultures most people's social behaviour is largely determined by personal goals that overlap only slightly with the goals of collectives, such as the family, the

work group, the tribe, political allies, coreligionists, fellow countrymen, and the state. When a conflict arises between personal and group goals, it is considered acceptable for the individual to place personal goals ahead of collective goals. By contrast, in collectivist cultures social behaviour is determined largely by goals shared with some collective, and if there is a conflict between personal and group goals, it is considered socially desirable to place collective goals ahead of personal goals.[49]

Additionally, the philosophic influence of Confucianism has been a pervasive influence among the Chinese people from ancient to contemporary times.[50] Confucianism inculcates and reinforces familial and group objectives. The values cherished are those of co-operation and collaboration, hierarchy and harmony, peace and stability. Confucianism stresses upon the five cardinal relationships which are viewed in a hierarchical order: that between emperor (the 'state' in modern parlance) and subject, father and son, husband and wife, elder brother and younger brother, and friend and friend.[51] As Cohen rightly remarks, the emphasis of Confucian values is 'not on the rights of the individual but the functioning of the social order, the maintenance of the group'.[52] The Confucianist philosophy, as such, is compatible with the ideals of collectivism.[53] Therefore, instead of seeking external agencies in the enforcement of one's rights, the Confucian collectivist is far more likely to look within the group membership to obtain social harmony as the paramount goal.[54] Any disturbance of this harmony is viewed unkindly by the other members of the group. It can be surmised from this aspect that the pursuit of individual rights is subsumed within the larger social good of maintaining group harmony.

In this connection, there are a number of social sanctions derived from customary norms which operate as effective social control mechanisms.[55] It is in this light that the Chinese are seen to downplay legal rules, particularly in civil (i.e. personal or private) matters. However, this is not to say that the law bears no significance for the Chinese. Rather, the law is seen as playing *a* role, rather than *the* role, in the usual regulation of human affairs. The emphasis, then, is diverted from the Rule of Law in Western culture to that of the Rule of 'Man' by an ethical ruler in Chinese culture.[56] As Confucius postulated, 'to govern (*cheng*) is to correct (*cheng*). If you set an example by being correct, who would dare to remain incorrect?'[57]

Quite naturally then, in the Chinese context, disputes are generally to be shunned.[58] This is because disputes fundamentally disturb their very desire for social harmony. Litigation basically runs counter to this, and is thereby to be avoided. The following is incisive:

> The Master said, 'In hearing litigation, I am no different from any other man. But if you insist on a difference, it is, perhaps, that I try to get the parties not to resort to litigation in the first place.[59]

It is little wonder that the pervasive teachings of Confucius have left the traditional Chinese with a non-litigious outlook. The Chinese methods of dealing with inevitable disputes lie in conciliation or mediation. In fact, one may go so far as to observe that with the Chinese, it is dispute *dissolution* rather than dispute resolution which they hold dear.[60] For instance, studies have shown that, 'Among Chinese, one of the responsibilities of those in positions of power is to anticipate and defuse potential confrontations'.[61] And, to quote Hsiao, 'in the tradition of imperial China, somewhat greater importance was consistently attached to prevention of conflicts before they arose than to ways and means of resolving them after they had broken out'.[62] Similarly, David and Brierly comment thus: 'contestations and disputes must be *dissolved* rather than *resolved* or decided ...'.[63] This phenomenon is supported by yet another observation:

> A more striking feature of Chinese commercial behaviour is the desire, ... to avoid acknowledging that a serious dispute exists at all, not only due to the cultural patterns, and Chinese bureaucratic habits but due also to a genuine desire to make disputes 'disappear'.[64]

In modern day China, for instance, there is a popular political slogan which states: 'combine mediation and prevention, and give primacy to prevention'.[65] Further, there exists an expectation that '[m]ediators are supposed not only to resolve disputes but also to prevent their occurrence'.[66] It may be asserted that the cultural leanings of the Chinese support such an observation.

It would not be wrong to say that there is a *natural tendency*, as propelled by one's culture, to pre-select mentally the disputing method, whether or not one *actually* engages in it. This is because in reality one's choices may be circumscribed by a variety of factors, e.g. the costs and expenses involved may be prohibitive, and there may be no certainty of winning the lawsuit. Westerners are still far more likely than the Chinese to *think* about litigation even though research findings in the West suggest that litigation represents a marginal disputing activity.[67]

As a corollary, disputes bear a personal aspect in individualistic cultures and a communal one in collectivist cultures. This point will be elaborated in the succeeding section.

Mediation Features

The above observations on cultural divergence give rise to interesting comparisons between modern Western mediation and traditional Chinese mediation. I shall focus on the issues of (i) conflict perception, i.e. whether a conflict is seen as personal or communitarian, (ii) voluntarism and the related considerations of party autonomy and the consensual theory, and (iii) conflict resolution in the form of a compromise.

Conflict perception. A dispute, in the Western sense, is often characterized as personal to the disputants concerned. This feature is again reflective of individualism. An individual is responsible for his or her own problems, and the problem is regarded as exclusive to him or her alone. Outside interference in the form of unsolicited assistance is discouraged. Rarely is a party who is a complete outsider be made privy to the dispute outside of a professional engagement. For instance, a Western mediator waits to be invited to mediate a dispute, in contradistinction with a Chinese mediator who can initiate or intercede a mediation at will.[68] In fact, the commonly heard phrase, 'This is none of your business!' is symptomatic of an individualistic culture. In this context, the conflict, which has been begun by the disputants in question, is a conflict between the immediate relevant parties: they and they alone. It is then their personal choice as to whether to consult a third party, or seek professional advice on how to deal with the problem at hand.

In contrast, first of all, as we recall, the Chinese tend to shun disputes. Any perceived disagreement causes some measure of personal discomfort. And, in the inevitable event of a dispute arising between two Chinese parties, the dispute almost always becomes communitarian in perspective. This is because in the Chinese collectivist culture, nothing is really personal, and everything seems to be communal, disputes included. Even though a dispute may essentially affect the immediate parties concerned, the collectivistic Chinese would tend to view it as affecting the group rather than being confined to the particular disputants.[69] By this is meant that a dispute may have started between the immediate relevant parties, but it, just as quickly, can escalate to communal proportions. For instance, a potential marriage breakdown between a couple is not viewed as the province of the couple alone. Rather, the problem becomes the pre-occupation of the two families concerned as well as the community at large.[70] True, in Western cultures, it is not uncommon for the in-laws to have some form of involvement. However, there is very little, if any, participation by members of the extended family (uncles, aunts, grandparents and so on), something, which, in contrast, commonly occurs among the Chinese. Every effort is directed at safeguarding the reputation and social standing of the families in the community and attempts at reconciliation are primarily geared towards this consideration rather than the couple's romantic feelings for one another. Very often, the fear of 'losing face' in the community militates against the couple's own wishes for a separation or ultimately, a divorce.[71]

Voluntarism. In an individualist culture, the Westerner sees the submission of a dispute to mediation as a voluntary exercise.[72] In the words of commentators, 'voluntarism is an essential component of mediation'[73] and 'voluntarism is the foremost tenet of good mediation'.[74] This requirement for voluntarism appears to be critical to the Western-style approach to mediation. In my opinion, culturally, for the Westerners, it has to appear to be so. This is because voluntarism is reflective of the ideals of individualism. The individualistic people are inclined to pursue their idealized and much-worshipped goals of the freedom of action, a characteristic individualistic trait.

This sense of voluntarism also gives rise to the perception of party autonomy which is regarded as critical to the success of mediation as a means of resolving disputes in Western culture. The individualistic person would regard as scornful anything that has to be procured with force, coercion or compulsion against one's will, as it were. As such, in the West, one's submission to mediation must be perceived of as an exercise of one's free choice and free will.

Therefore, the mediation process has to be consensual, in theory at least.

In light of the communitarian nature of most Chinese disputes, there is an ever-present pressure on the disputing parties to settle them as quickly and as quietly as possible. There is a popular Chinese saying to the effect that 'family ignominy should not be published to the outsider'.[75] As such, Chinese disputants have an obligation to mediate, in order that the dispute may be dealt with expeditiously and in a private manner. Such an obligation may be seen in contradistinction with the Western disputant who can purport to choose whether or not to mediate, who then exercises his or her right to mediate accordingly. The notion of a voluntary choice is there for the Western disputant, although her practical choice may be limited by circumstances. The important difference is that, in theory at least, there exists such a personal choice, which is concordant with individualistic orientations.

The Chinese party does not appear to enjoy such a personal liberty. Often, he or she is compelled to mediate by the larger society to which he or she belongs. Peace and stability and harmony are the societal goals. Individual disagreements are seen as disruptive of such goals and must be dissipated in the interests of the good of all. Mediation, seen in this light, is imposed and involuntary. This is because whether the Chinese disputants like it or not, there is a cultural obligation for them to mediate the dispute. The end of the personal dispute serves the crucial objective of achieving and maintaining social harmony. The collectivists are interested in group goals, and the personal welfare of the individual is secondary to them.[76] The practice of mediation definitely serves the interests of the group as its attempts at dispute settlement are more subtle, more non-confrontational, indirect and more amicable, and they serve to uphold communal peace and unity.

Conflict resolution and compromise. What is regarded as a necessary corollary for Western conflict resolution is the vindication of personal justice, which is reflected in litigation. The pursuit of justice is an entrenched and well-cherished individual right. The aims of legal institutions in Western culture serve this goal primarily. Individual rights should be preserved, protected and defended. The courts are the greatest guardians of any such breaches. Justice shall be done. However, in Western mediation, while the final outcome may bear some vindication of personal justice, it is heavily tempered with a compromise solution. The idea of mediation, therefore, is seen as rather incompatible with the goal of personal justice cherished by individualists. This is because mediation requires the parties to concede points, to compromise a little, and to live with mutually agreed solutions. It is not a win-lose situation nor is it a zero-sum game that litigants are so familiar with. Participants engaged in a Western-style mediation are instinctively geared towards a justice solution, although compromise is an, if not *the*, expected outcome. In fact, in light of Western individualism, research has proven a 'less tolerance for compromise'.[77]

In contrast, quite naturally, for the Chinese, the outcome of a mediation serves to restore group harmony; thus, a compromise solution is the ideal norm to achieve it.[78] It does not allow personal justice to interfere. Such is not the preoccupation of the collectivists. The success of a mediation is the extent to which the reparation of social harmony and restoration of group solidarity is made possible again. In the words of Triandis:

> The point is that in a society where harmony is the ideal and 'doing the right thing' is essential for good relations, one often does what one believes to be socially desirable even if one's attitudes are inconsistent with the action.[79]

Unlike the case with the individualistic Westerner, the attainment of individual justice is not as important a goal in a Chinese-style mediation as is the preservation of group harmony.[80] This outcome is in accordance with their social obligation to mediate and consistent with the collectivists' objectives. As such, compromises are regarded as acceptable solutions and more readily implemented by the Chinese parties. The tendency and ability to compromise is a well-known facet of Chinese Confucianism.

Mediation Challenges

It is my contention that in spite of the popularity of the mediation movement in the West, the idea of mediation is not *culturally* acceptable to the Westerner ingrained and imbued with individualistic ideals. Western individualism goes hand-in-glove with litigation. Mediation has come to exist in the West without, it would appear, certain cultural imperatives as found in the East. Thus, in the West, there seems to be a perceived need for a theory to fill the cultural void.[81] Mediation in the West has proven popular mainly on the grounds of expediency. Contrasted with litigation, it is perceived as quick, informal and more amenable to personal control.[82]

There are some assumptions in Chinese mediation which are absent in Western mediation which may pose as challenges in this cross-cultural study. I identify these main challenges as follows: (i) the difficulty of a compromise solution and the voluntary enforcement of the mediated award, and (ii) the mediator role. I shall deal with them in turn.

Award enforcement.   Individualism promotes a zero-sum approach to conflict resolution. As raised above, a compromise solution requires Western disputants to meet half way and this goes against their basic notions of justice. Justice may not be compromised. Therefore, although the use of mediation is an efficient way of resolving a problem, its ultimate solution may not be culturally agreeable. Furthermore, if the compromise award is unsatisfactory, the disputants may still be at liberty to ignore it and go about their own ways, resulting in inevitable litigation. The voluntary enforcement of a mediated award may pose to be a problem because of the likelihood of non-compliance as a result of a lack of social pressures.[83] In this connection, studies have demonstrated that the successful settlement rates in the West rank lower when compared with those in China.[84]

As far as the Chinese are concerned, the idea of mediation is culturally acceptable to them, theoretically and philosophically attributable to collectivism and Confucianism which emphasize communal values. Sociologically, they are used to the idea of compromise.

Generally speaking, Chinese disputants do not have a problem with the non-enforcement of awards due to prevailing social sanctions. If a disputant does not abide by an award, she is seen as not giving face to the mediator.[85] Such an action bears strong social repercussions, and the recalcitrant may be ostracized by the community, the heaviest penalty of all. In this regard, the use of face-saving as a cultural sanction is a strong one. This is because the mediation is seen as an activity conducted in the interests of the community, and the community, therefore, has a vested interest to see to it that an award rendered or solution proposed is implemented or complied with. The individual disputant may not like the outcome, but has little say in it if the desires of the community prevail. Again, this cultural trait is concordant with collectivism.

The mediator.   The role of the mediator, as mentioned earlier, also differs in Western and Chinese senses.

> The Chinese mediator does not merely act as a channel of communication between the disputants; he is expected to propose possible solutions, to explain the framework of law within which the agreement must be reached, and to take an important part in the parties' negotiations.[86]

The Chinese mediator acts within the cultural expectations of being a figure higher in status, who is seen as authoritative, instructive, educative, and who bears a social responsibility for maintaining peace, unity, order and stability.[87]

In comparison, the above suggests that the Chinese mediators traditionally play a far greater role. They can be interventionist, pro-active, and maybe even dictatorial. They can certainly be expected to be authoritarian. Because they command general social respect when appointed as mediators, the Chinese disputants look up to them as such. Again, this phenomenon is concordant with a collectivist approach to disputing and conflict-solving, as delved upon earlier. To quote Palmer:

> In resolving disputes a Chinese mediator is expected not only to help the parties reach a settlement that accords with their wishes but also to promote important socio-political values and policies.[88]

In a similar vein, Wolski points out that the monetary rewards for the Chinese mediators are paltry, if at all, and yet they are expected to perform their duties on call,[89] and for these mediators, the rewards are in the form of 'social prestige of good face and the fulfilment of their social role (*li*)'.[90] Indeed, in the context of Chinese collectivism-Confucianism, these assertions make sense.

Because of the private and public mediator functions in the Chinese case, it is usual for a mediator to be a person known personally to the disputants. In fact, often, this is seen as a desired pre-requisite.[91] It also serves to import mutual trust between the mediator and the disputants. Such a mediator can bring his personal knowledge of the parties, their circumstances, and most importantly, their relationships, to the conflict matrix. It is also in this light that the Chinese notions of *guanxi, ganqing,* and *renqing* can operate effectively.[92] Due to the fact that the Chinese mediator can enforce moral values and educate the disputants,[93] his integrity is, therefore, unquestioned and the disputants do not then perceive any sense of bias or prejudice or doubt his neutrality. It is a loss of the mediator's face if the disputants were to even faintly conceive of these issues.

In sharp contrast, the above mediator attributes can hardly be said to be requirements of Western mediators whose role is primarily to resolve, or to facilitate the resolving of, the conflict between the immediate disputants. The Western mediators are primarily regarded as facilitators. They do not, and are not expected to, shoulder the responsibility of espousing social values.[94]

Furthermore, the neutrality of the Western mediator is regarded as essential. In direct contrast with the Chinese, if the mediator is personally known to either disputant, his or her independence is questioned. There is a suspicion of bias. Such a mediator normally declines to mediate the dispute for want of neutrality. As such, convention requires that Western mediators are 'complete strangers'[95] to the parties and the proceedings.

It may be said that the requirements of mediator independence, neutrality and impartiality in Western-style mediation are reflective of individualistic principles. The fact that a Western mediator's role is confined to resolving the dispute at hand rather than assuming a wider social responsibility is testimony to individualist ideals.

Conclusion

In the East and in the West, the dictates of the predominant cultures appear to pre-select the conflict strategies. If a culture is pre-dominantly collectivistic, group or communal goals are emphasized. Conversely, in a pre-dominantly individualistic culture, the personal goals override the social objectives. In conflict resolution, Triandis refers to Ting-Toomey's predictions as follows,

> ...individualists will be more concerned with saving their own face, autonomy, domination, control, and solutions to the problem; they will use direct negotiation strategies. By

contrast, collectivists will be more concerned with saving face for the other or for both, approval, being obliging and smooth, and avoiding conflict. They will use indirect negotiation strategies – for example, they will welcome mediators.[96]

'A rose by any other name smells as sweet,' so writes the famous and timeless bard, William Shakespeare.[97] However, the same may not be said of the term 'mediation' in the cross-cultural (Sino-Western) context. As eluded to above, the use of mediation may sound alike across borders and across cultures. However, it would be a mistake to suppose that it is *exactly* the same in the different cultural environments. This comment is more true when one compares and contrasts traditional Chinese mediation and the more modern forms of Western-style mediation. In short, traditional Chinese mediation is vertically structured whereas Western-style mediation is meant to be horizontally based. This observation reflects the collectivism-individualism dimension.[98] In another instance, the Western approach to mediation tends to be rights-based and the Chinese style is predominantly obligations-based, with these features again being reflective of the individualism-collectivism variant.[99] In light of this, culture does play a pivotal role in shaping the perceptual and procedural aspects of mediation, rendering its respective processes with a particular hue and moulding them in a specific style. One may concede that, ultimately, mediation serves the purpose of dispute resolution in a compromise-seeking, amicable and largely non-confrontational way. But the reality is that there are present cultural factors which contribute to the various subtle and apparent differences of mediation practices in the East and in the West. In the Australian context, this cross-cultural appreciation of mediation is significant as indigenous communities' experience of mediation resembles that of the Chinese model. It would, therefore, be wrong, if not, dangerous, to impose the Western style of mediation on the indigenous communities when the cultures of mainstream Australians differ from those of the indigenous cultures.[100]

A further important point to note is that a cross-cultural study of this nature, like most comparative work, serves the useful purposes of understanding how and why people behave in particular ways. There should be no judgment call on which is better, but, rather, on what are different. Indeed, through an understanding of such differences one would then be enabled to transcend the cultural barriers which tend to impede effective human communication and interaction.

In the succeeding Chapters, I shall attempt to examine the non-litigious outlook of the Chinese by tracing their cultural tradition including their attitude towards Law, abhorrence for the formal justice system, preference for informal dispute settlement, and the underlying enabling factors. The Chinese reputation for mediation has fascinated the West for a long time. Even if modern mediation as now practised in the People's Republic of China represents a departure from the traditional versions, I would argue that traditional Chinese mediation is still worthy of study in that it has helped to entrench mediation in Chinese culture, is continually perpetuated by the various global Chinese communities (particularly in the rural regions), and bears testimony to the time-tested Chinese Confucian heritage.

NOTES

[1]   A Chinese proverb.

[2]   See William B. Gudykunst, *Bridging Differences: Effective Intergroup Communication*, Sage Publications, Thousand Oaks (California), 1994 (second edition), at page 197.

[3]   Laurence Boulle, *Mediation: Skills and Techniques*, Butterworths, Sydney, 2001, at page 9; Laurence Boulle, *Mediation: Principles, Process, Practice*, Butterworths, Sydney, 1996, at pages 42-43. See also, Peter Condliffe, *Conflict Management: a practical guide*, TAFE Publications, Melbourne, 1991, at page 16.

[4]   Laurence Boulle (2001), note 3 above, at page 9.

[5]   See Elizabeth Weldon and Karen A. Jehn, 'Conflict Management in US-Chinese Joint Ventures' (1995) Carnegie Bosch Institute Working Paper 95-10, http://cbi.gsia.cmu.edu/

[6]   Sally Engle Merry, "Book Review: Disputing Without Culture", (1987) 100 Harvard Law Review 2057, at page 2063.

[7]   Hilary Astor and Christine M Chinkin, *Dispute Resolution In Australia*, Butterworths, Sydney, 1992, at page 1.

[8]   Michael Palmer, 'The Revival of Mediation in the People's Republic of China' in W.E. Butler (ed), *Yearbook on Socialist Legal Systems: 1987*, Transnational Publishers, Inc., Dobbs Ferry, New York, 1988, at page 220.

9   See Bobette Wolski, 'Voluntarism and Consensuality: Defining Charactersitics of Mediation?' (1996-1997) 15 *Australian Bar Review* 213, at page 218.

10   For some definitions of 'culture', see GOH Bee Chen, *Negotiating With The Chinese*, Dartmouth Publishing Company, Aldershot, 1996, at pages 17-18; William B. Gudykunst, note 2 above, at pages 35-37.

11   Hilary Astor and Christine M Chinkin, note 7 above, at page 5.

12   Laurence Boulle (1996), note 3 above, at page 32.

13   See Laurence Boulle (1996), note 3 above, at pages 32-33; Hilary Astor and Christine M. Chinkin, note 7 above, at page 20.

14   Laurence Boulle (1996), note 3 above, at page 33.

15   See Josefina Muniz Rendon, 'When You Can't Get Through to Them: Cultural Diversity In Mediation', http://www.mediate.com/articles/rendon.cfm

16   Edward T. Hall, *Beyond Culture*, Anchor Books/Doubleday, New York, 1976, 1981, at page 162.

17   See Elizabeth Weldon and Karen A. Jehn, note 5 above.

18   See Dean Barnlund, *Public and Private Self in Japan and the United States*, Simul, Tokyo, 1975, at page 423, quoted in William B. Gudykunst, note 2 above, at page 198.

19   Stanley B. Lubman and Gregory C. Wajnowski, 'International Commercial Dispute Resolution in China: A Practical Assessment' (1993) 4 *The American Review of International Arbitration* 107, at page 112.

20   William B. Gudykunst, note 2 above, at page 198.

21   Reg Little and Warren Reed, *The Confucian Renaissance*, The Federation Press, Sydney, 1989, at page 83.

22   William B. Gudykunst, note 2 above, at page 197.

23   Similar observations are made by Donald C. Clarke in "Dispute Resolution In China" (1991) *Journal of Chinese Law*, at pages 245-296.

24   Donald C. Clarke, note 23 above, at page 294.

25   Michael J. Moser, *Law and Social Change in a Chinese Community: A Case Study From Rural Taiwan*, Oceana Publications, Inc., London, 1982, at page 2.

26   Individualists and collectivists have been encouraged to manage conflicts by taking into account their respective cultural differences: see William B. Gudykunst, note 2 above, at pages 205-206.

27   GOH Bee Chen, note 10 above, at pages 24-25.

28   See Elizabeth Weldon and Karen A. Jehn, note 5 above.

29   William B. Gudykunst, note 2 above, at page 43; GOH Bee Chen, note 10 above, at pages 24-25.

30   See Peter Condliffe, note 3 above, at page 9.

31   See Stanley B. Lubman and Gregory C. Wajnowski, note 19 above, at page 115.

32   Geert Hofstede, *Cultures and Organizations: Intercultural Cooperation and its Importance for Survival*, HarperCollins Publishers, 1994, at page 58.

33   GOH Bee Chen, note 10 above, at pages 27-29.

34   GOH Bee Chen, note 10 above, at pages 27-29; William B. Gudykunst, note 2 above, at pages 40-41.

35   Elizabeth Weldon and Karen A. Jehn, note 5 above.

36   See Edward T. Hall, *The Silent Language*, Greenwood Press, Westport (Connecticut), 1959.

37   Jerold S. Auerbach, *Justice Without Law*, Oxford University Press, New York/Oxford, 1983, at page 10.

38   Reg Little and Warren Reed, note 21 above, at pages 83-84.

39   Jerold S. Auerbach, note 37 above, at page 10.

40   Elizabeth Weldon and Karen A. Jehn, note 5 above.

41   GOH Bee Chen, note 10 above, at pages 24-27.

42   GOH Bee Chen, note 10 above, at pages 24-27; William B. Gudykunst, note 2 above, at pages 40-41.

43   Francis L.K. Hsu, *Americans and Chinese: Passage to Differences*, University of Hawaii Press, Honolulu, 1981 (third edition), at page 135.

44   William B. Gudykunst, note 2 above, at page 41.

45   GOH Bee Chen, note 10 above, at page 25.

46   William B. Gudykunst, note 2 above, at page 41.

47   Geert Hofstede, note 32 above, at pages 66-67; William B. Gudykunst, note 2 above, at page 41.

48   William B. Gudykunst, note 2 above, at page 41.

49   Harry C. Triandis, 'Cross-Cultural Studies of Individualism and Collectivism' in John J. Berman (ed), *Nebraska Symposium on Motivation 1989: Cross-Cultural Perspectives*, University of Nebraska Press, Lincoln and London, 1990, at page 42. Also quoted in GOH Bee Chen, note 10 above, at page 23.

50   GOH Bee Chen, note 10 above, at page 50.

51   *Chung-Yung*, or *The Doctrine of the Mean*. XX:8. See also GOH Bee Chen, note 10 above, at page 26; Michael Bond and Kwang-Kuo Hwang, 'The Social Psychology of the Chinese People' in Michael Harris Bond (ed), *The Psychology of the Chinese People*, Oxford University Press, Hong Kong, 1986, at page 216; Tu Wei-Ming, *Centrality and Commonality: An Essay on Confucian Religiousness*, State University of New York Press, Albany, 1989, at page 54.

52   Jerome A. Cohen, 'Chinese Mediation on the Eve of Modernization' (1966) 54 *California Law Review*, at page 1207. See also Mark Elvin, *Changing Stories in the Chinese World*, Stanford University Press, Stanford, 1997, at page 33.

53   See also Michael Harris Bond and Kwang-Kuo Hwang, note 51 above, at page 262.

54   GOH Bee Chen, note 10 above, at page 70.

55   See Chapter 4 below.

56   See Reg Little and Warren Reed, note 21 above, at page 83; Lester Ross, 'The Changing Profile of Dispute Resolution in Rural China: The Case of Zouping County, Shandong' (1989) 26 *Stanford Journal of International Law* 15, at pages 15-17.

57   *The Analects*, Book XII: 17. See D.C. Lau (translated), *Confucius: The Analects*, Penguin Books, London, 1979, at page 115. See also Lucie Cheng and Arthur Rosett, 'Contract With A Chinese Face: Socially Embedded Factors In The Transformation From Hierarchy To Market, 1978-1989' (1991) 5 *Journal of Chinese Law* 143, at pages 157-158.

58   GOH Bee Chen, note 10 above, at page 70. See also Michael Harris Bond and Kwang-Kuo Hwang, note 51 above, at page 262.

59   *The Analects*, Book XII: 13. See D.C. Lau, note 57 above, at page 115.

60   GOH Bee Chen, note 10 above, at page 70.

61   Michael Harris Bond and Kwang-Kuo Hwang, note 51 above, at page 262.

62   Kung-Chuan Hsiao, *Compromise In Imperial China*, School of International Studies, University of Washington, Seattle, 1979, at page 36.

63   Rene David and John E. C. Brierley, *Major Legal Systems Of The World Today*, Stevens & Sons, London, 1985 (3rd edition), at page 518.

64   Stanley B. Lubman and Gregory C. Wajnowski, note 19 above, a t page 115.

65   Michael Palmer, note 8 above, at page 235. See also the same work at page 252.

66   Michael Palmer, note 8 above, at page 244.

67   Hilary Astor and Christine M Chinkin, note 7 above, at page 29.

68   Bobette Wolski, 'Culture, Society and Mediation in China and the West' (1996-1997) 3 *Commercial Dispute Resolution Journal* 97, at pages 115-116.

69   See, for instance, Francis L.K. Hsu's theorizing of the Chinese concept of humanity, *ren*, as being based on 'the individual's transactions with his fellow human beings' quoted in Michael Harris Bond (ed), note 51 above, at page 220.

70   In this connection, Palmer cites an interesting and insightful mediation relating to a Chinese marriage breakdown which was saved by mediation. See Michael Palmer, note 8 above, at pages 250-251.

71   Weldon and Jehn offer interesting explanations on the differences in 'face-work' in collectivist and individualist cultures: see Elizabeth Weldon and Karen A. Jehn, note 5 above.

72   Laurence Boulle (1996), note 3 above, at pages 15-18.

73   R Ingleby, 'Compulsion Is Not The Answer' (1992) 27 *Australian Law News* 17, at page 18, quoted in Laurence Boulle (1996), note 3 above, at page 15.

74   P Adler, 'Resolving Public Policy Conflicts Through Mediation: The Water Roundtable' (1990) 1 *Australian Dispute Resolution Journal* 69, at page 78, quoted in Laurence Boulle (1996), note 3 above, at page 15.

75   *'Jia cho pu keh wai yang'*, a Chinese phrase translated by the author.

76   See Harry C Triandis, note 49 above, at page 80.

77   Harry C. Triandis, note 49 above, at page 83.

78   See generally Kung-Chuan Hsiao, note 62 above.

79   Harry C Triandis, note 49 above, at page 80.

80   See Michael J. Moser, note 25 above, at page 65.

81   See Laurence Boulle (1996), note 3 above, at page v.

82   Bobette Wolski, note 68 above, at pages 111-112.

83   Bobette Wolski, note 68 above, at page 122.

84   Bobette Wolski, note 68 above, at pages 121- 122. See also Ralph H. Folsom and John H. Minan (eds), *Law in the People's Republic*

of China: Commentary, Readings and Materials, Martinus Nijhoff Publishers, Dordrecht, 1989, at page 85.

85   See Michael Palmer, note 8 above, at page 263.

86   Michael Palmer, note 8 above, at page 244.

87   Michael Palmer, note 8 above, at pages 224 and 244.

88   Michael Palmer, note 8 above, at page 258.

89   Bobette Wolski, note 68 above, at page 113.

90   L W Do, 'Dispute-Settlement in Chinese-American Communities' (1973) 21 *American Journal of Comparative Law* 627, quoted in Bobette Wolski, note 68 above, at page 113.

91   See Roderick W. Macneil, 'Contract in China: Law, Practice and Dispute Resolution' (1986) *Stanford Law Review* 303, at page 329.

92   These notions will be elaborated as social sanctions in Chapter 3 below.

93   See Michael Palmer, note 8 above, at pages 225-226, and 247; Jerome A. Cohen, note 52 above, at pages 1224-1225.

94   Bobette Wolski, note 68 above, at page 121.

95   Bobette Wolski, note 68 above, at page 114.

96   Harry C. Triandis, note 49 above, at page 91, referring to S Ting-Toomey, *Intercultural Conflict Styles: A face-negotiation theory*, paper presented at the meetings of the International Communications Association, New Orleans, LA, May 1988.

97   William Shakespeare in *Romeo And Juliet*.

98   Harry C. Triandis, note 49 above, at page 72.

99   See, for example, Jeswald W. Salacuse, 'So, What Is The Deal Anyway? Contracts and Relationships as Negotiating Goals' (1998) *Negotiation Journal* 5, at page 11; Ralph H. Folsom and John H. Minan (eds), note 84 above, at page 86.

100   See, for example, Australian Law Reform Commission, *Review of the Adversarial System of Litigation: ADR – its role in federal dispute resolution*, Issues Paper 25, Canberra, June 1998, at pages 78-79.

2 Chinese Legal Thinking

The thing is we should make it our aim that there not be any lawsuits at all.[1]

Introduction

It is almost always surprising to learn that with a civilization as ancient as that of the Chinese, the legal system has never assumed as prominent a role as it has in the West. In Western culture, it is a normal tendency to think that the legal system underpins our day-to-day existence. The formal law is so much a part of our modern lifestyle that it is unthinkable to separate oneself from the legal implications of one's actions. For example, a solicitous shoe salesman knocks on your front door and you end up signing a contract by the time he makes his exit. You regret this within twenty-four hours. Depending on jurisdictions, there may or may not be a cooling-off period for such contractual obligations to become binding on the parties. Usually, though, the average lay person tends to think that he or she is bound by the contract and has to go through with the purchase. This simple example illustrates how easily our daily lives can get entangled with the operation of the formal legal system.

The way in which we handle disputes bears a direct relationship with our perception of how the formal legal system makes an impact on our lives. Additionally, the Common Law Justice system subscribes to an adversarial style of litigation which tends to produce a zero-sum game. In the pursuit of individual rights and justice, the natural result is that one party must win and the other must lose. There is nothing in between. The court system, therefore, produces a successful litigant and a disappointed one. Litigiousness has been a hallmark of the Western legal system for centuries.

The above is in contrast with the Chinese outlook which is more comfortable with the ideals of compromise and harmony. The Chinese are generally looked upon as a non-litigious people. For instance, with regard to the Chinese in Malaysia, a former Lord President of Malaysia, the late Tun Mohamed Suffian Hashim, shared this with me at a private interview: 'the Chinese (in Malaysia) are practical people. They believe in reconciliation rather than confrontation'.[2] Such an insight can generally be found in legal literature to do with Chinese law. The aversion to the formal legal system is considered a hallmark Chinese experience. Litigation is shunned where disputes are concerned. The preference for conciliation or mediation in the way of dispute resolution is a strikingly familiar feature in Chinese culture. As asserted in the earlier Chapter, in the case of the Chinese, it is not a matter of dispute resolution, but dispute dissolution.[3] To recall, the distinction between the two rests with the notion that, in the latter situation, every effort is made by all the parties concerned to prevent a dispute from even arising in the very first place. It may be said that the idea of dispute dissolution is attractive to, and in accordance with, Chinese culture which has, for long, emphasized the inherent values of inter-personal relationships. Such relationships ought to be cultivated, maintained and preserved. Conflicts or disputes are viewed as hostile disturbances to such inter-personal associations. Therefore, the ability to dissolve a dispute rather than to resolve a dispute may be said to be a cultural high point for the Chinese. Furthermore, dispute dissolution avoids the necessity for confrontation. This aids the facilitation of the maintenance of social harmony, a much desired community goal.[4]

Certainly, one may attribute the desire for conflict avoidance to the Chinese insistence on the idea of *ho*, or harmony. In fact, every member of a Chinese Confucian society strives for harmony in his or her daily existence. Basically, *ho* implies the element of compromise, or 'being at one with one's immediate environment'.[5] Seen in the light of disputes, it is about meeting the other party midway, not exacting one's justice, fulfilling one's role in a community which cherishes the group above oneself. Undoubtedly, this idea of harmony in both the personal and social contexts has been the basis for the Chinese way of life.

Needless to say, the Chinese idea of harmony in the maintenance of social order appears to differ from the Western legal outlook. In the West, the maintenance of social order is a function of the legal system, and control institutions are characteristic features necessary for the operation of law.[6] This difference was perhaps what prompted Dennis Lloyd to remark that 'the Chinese never succeeded in developing a scientific outlook on the Western pattern, which presupposes the acceptance of pre-ordained laws'.[7]

Tradition, to a large extent, has played a part in influencing the behaviour of the Chinese in the contemporary world. This statement is, perhaps, more true with reference to the rural Chinese in general. This is because the Chinese in the villages represent a more cohesive social group. Their fondness for perpetuating traditional customs is still much evident.[8] In any event, it is relevant to trace the legal tradition of Imperial China in order to enable one to understand why the Chinese have been known generally for their non-litigiousness. Such knowledge will also enable one to understand why the practice of mediation in conflict resolution has had a flourishing impact on Chinese society as a whole.

The Traditional Chinese Concept of Law And Justice

In traditional China, the formal law was implemented to protect the rights of the state rather than the individual. The law was seen as an instrument of state power, designed to shield the bureaucracy from the common people, rather than as a mechanism for the individual person to redress personal wrongs. In this regard, one could view the function of the law and the overall legal system as a guardian of the state, which might have little to do in the actual regulation of the lives of the subjects *inter se*. Moreover, China had, from early times, possessed a kind of bureaucracy. The government of state affairs was heavily centralized. This could be seen from the extensive official control of the life of the peasantry.[9]

Interestingly enough, there also appeared to be no provision for the civil law in early Chinese legislation.[10] That was because the law in traditional China concerned itself chiefly with the criminal and administrative matters since the laws passed were essentially penal in nature and official or bureaucratic in character. Such a form of promulgation necessarily entailed a usurpation of individual liberty so that state power could be consolidated and state authority could be unquestionably exercised. This feature again reflects the idea and the conception of law in the traditional Chinese society as being state-centred, and not directed for the benefit of the common folk. In this connection, one may note what van der Sprenkel states in relation to Chinese law, 'Law, equated with a system of punishments, was in its nature harsh and to be avoided by reasonable men'.[11] It may be remarked that such an observation is hardly surprising. This is largely due to the fact that the existence of the law in the traditional Chinese society was seen by the populace as both penal and authoritarian, used more as a punitive tool by the state vis-a-vis the subject, and highly regulatory. An individual subject caught entangled in the machinery of the law would feel trapped, stifled and strangled, and would want little or nothing to do with it. This is quite unlike in the West whereby the law has traditionally been portrayed as capable of liberating one from one's troubles and may be used as an instrument to champion one's rights. The perception of law in Western culture idealizes the individual as the main actor, and the role of the state as the executor of the collective will. The reverse, so it seemed, was true of ancient China.

Earlier, I touched upon the concept of harmony and its anchor feature in the Chinese way of life. The concept of harmony represented one of the cardinal principles of *li*[12] taught by Confucius in contradistinction to the Legalist School in Imperial China which gave rise to a system of positive law, *fa*.[13] It has been suggested that 'a comparison may be made between Confucian *li* and the Western concept of natural law in apposition to a comparison between Legalist *fa* and Western positive law'.[14]

Essentially, Law was to the Chinese mind nothing more than the imposition of fines and penalties for official transgression.[15] Chinese Legal literature was thus considered unworthy of study on 'aesthetic or inspirational' grounds owing to its 'utilitarian' purpose.[16] Undeniably, China had endeavoured to produce impressive legal codes, for instance, the *Ta Ch'ing Lu Li* compiled during the Qing Dynasty (1644-1911). Despite this, the traditional Chinese society was not a legally-oriented one. This could be due to the general phenomenon, as described by van der Sprenkel, that 'much of Chinese social organization had a legal aspect'.[17]

The dominance of criminality in Chinese legislation has been succinctly commented upon by Phillip M. Chen:

> Through the entire history of China, the imperial dynasties, after seizing government power with military force, always took the enactment of law as their foremost task in order to suppress the resistance and to preserve their dominance. In ancient China, the so-called 'law' was nothing but criminal code, because in those days *fa* (law) meant *hsing*

(punishment), and the Imperial law was in effect, criminal law.[18]

As such, China not only has a legal system, it seems to be about one of the most ancient ones in existence.[19] The irony is that despite the existence of an ancient and mature legal system in traditional China, law has never been placed upon the pedestal of the Chinese way of life. Generally speaking, for the Chinese, moral precepts, ethical norms, and socially-approved rules meant much more than legal sanctions as the prime force in compelling obedience. This observation is particularly true in civil disputes.

Some of the reasons which may be accountable for this general aversion to the formal law suggested by Phillip M. Chen are:

1.   As noted earlier, China possessed a bureaucratic system of government whose style of governing impinged upon the affairs of the common people, exemplified by and large by the peasantry. The lives of the peasantry were inextricably intertwined with the affairs of the state. As history would have it, this early bureaucratic state of China had begun to make use of the law as an instrument for keeping social order, but by punitive means. In this regard, the law was definitely seen as being more concerned with state affairs than with the regulation of the lay person's life. Not surprisingly, the law bore strong negative overtones for the common people.

2.   Confucianism had always been a pervasive factor in the Chinese worldview. Confucianism was viewed not merely as a valuable stream of Chinese philosophy, but, more importantly, it was a practical legacy and incorporated as part and parcel of the ordinary day-to-day life of the peasantry. The inculcation of Confucian values and ethics definitely put law in an unfavourable and inferior position. There were in existence various other social groups such as the clan associations, business guilds and families which played a constructive role in the dispute settlement process. This, in turn, reduced the necessity for recourse to the official law.

3.   There were well-known perils associated with litigation: corruption was rampant in the administration of a justice system which was fraught with malpractices; court-houses were situated far from the residence of the disputants, the magistrates were said to be 'corrupt, cruel and lazy';[20] trials were considered humiliating and

the frequent delays often resulted in a miscarriage of justice.

4.　　　Quite unlike, for example, the English legal system in which an individual can defend himself or herself, the Chinese legal system did not possess the adversarial tradition. A person who was unfortunate enough to be involved in litigation would almost always feel helpless and vulnerable. This is because, when brought before the court, the defendant had to rely solely on 'the tender mercies of officialdom'.[21]

The following summarizes the traditional Chinese attitude towards the Law. Much of it is true even today:

> The law played a limited role in society mainly because the law, essentially a penal code, included very few provisions on family, marriage, adoption, inheritance, property and debts. In fact, the law dealt mainly with violations and the penalties for such violations. Many of these matters, which could be considered civil laws in modern concepts, were very much neglected and largely left to customs or *li* ... Moreover, litigation was discouraged. Since the law was punitive and since people were treated in a humiliating manner before the court, it was a disgrace to be involved in a legal case ... There was a tendency among the people to avoid litigation. They preferred to settle disputes outside the court. Many cases were settled within the family or *tsu*, the village or the guild. Elders and gentry members often acted as arbitrators. Only cases which failed to be settled by these means went to court.[22]

Legal Tradition

Chinese legal tradition can be traced to two major Schools of thought, to wit, Confucianism and Legalism.[23] On their respective themes, while Confucianism advocated a return to the study of antiquity in order to restore the traditional regard for order in the universe, Legalism was concerned with the consolidation of state power regardless of any detriment to individual liberty.[24] Essentially, Confucianism focussed upon personal ethics and morality in order to produce desirable behaviour. In contrast, Legalism placed primacy on objective rules and punishments to secure compliance. It may be asserted that the vastly different outcomes contributed by Confucianism and Legalism have had a lasting legacy for the Chinese in their attitudes towards the formal law and access to justice.

The Confucianist Philosophy

Confucius was the founder of this School of philosophy popularly known as Confucianism. Some sinologists have aptly commented, 'if we were to describe in one word the Chinese way of life for the last two thousand years, the word would be 'Confucian''.[25] This clearly portrays the significance and dominance of this School of thought in the traditional Chinese way of life.

The name 'Confucius' is actually the name expressed in the Latinized version of 'K'ung Fu-tzu' or 'Master K'ung', i.e. the title in Mandarin conferred on him in reverence. His surname was K'ung, and personal name Ch'iu.[26] He was said to have lived around the period 551-479 B.C.[27]

Generally speaking, the Chinese believed in the trinity of heaven, earth and humanity. The world of nature and the world of humanity were inextricably intertwined. In the Confucianist view, the natural harmony was reflected in the moral goodness of humanity. The individual was, therefore, taught to be morally disciplined so as not to upset the cosmic harmony. A disturbance of the cosmic harmony meant that human disasters might follow, and catastrophes might ensue.

In order to ensure a good, upright and moral upbringing, there was a very strong emphasis given to the role of education, particularly in the field of moral learning. Confucius himself believed that an education could alter one's behaviour and rectify one's nature. One of his famous sayings goes thus: 'a piece of jade cannot become an object of art without chiselling, and a man cannot come to know the moral law without education'.[28]

In relation to the Law, the Confucian theory upheld the view that human nature was inherently good. One was capable of deviant conduct only if one lacked guidance or was put in adverse circumstances: 'in the beginning, human nature is about the same. It is the social environment that makes the difference'.[29] Bad conduct referred to a departure from the age-old norms of acceptable behaviour, in accordance with *li*. Adherence to *li* was encouraged because '*li* prevents what is going to happen, while law [attempts to] prevent what has already happened'.[30] The Confucianists were concerned with the importance of observing filial piety, showing respect for the elders, being loyal and submissive to one's superiors, practising social propriety and being righteous in one's dealings with others. They argued that these virtues could not be dismissed as valid social engineering forces.

As previously noted, the value of education was recognized. Confucius maintained that the power of education lay in its ability 'to prevent evils before they occur and to arouse respect in trifling matters'.[31] Thus, the people were made to do good and to refrain from evil without being conscious of it. Confucius firmly believed that in order to prevent the commission of crimes or any other socially harmful behaviour, one must be taught a sense of values and be educated to know shame:

> The Master said, 'if you govern the people by laws, and keep them in order by penalties, they will avoid the penalties, yet lose their sense of shame. But if you govern them by your moral excellence, and keep them in order by your dutiful conduct, they will retain their sense of shame, and also live up to this standard'.[32]

This may be compared to what Lu Chia[33] said about the law, and its non-educative role: 'Law is used to punish the evil, not to encourage the good. The law is able to punish men, but unable to make men uncorrupt; it is able to kill men but is unable to make men kind'.[34]

Education was, therefore, in the Confucianist philosophy, desirable in cultivating virtue. Virtue could be cultivated through adherence to *li*, the key term of Confucian teaching. Confucius said that *li* was the guiding principle of the sage-rulers of antiquity which was formulated according to the laws of Heaven. The aim of *li* was to prescribe rules for proper human conduct.[35] The attainment of *li* was also important based on the philosophy that 'the work is Heaven's; it is man's to act'.[36] Thus, a ruler lacking in virtue would result in the mandate of Heaven being revoked. Chaos would then ensue.[37] As Confucius postulated:

> He who exercises government by means of his virtue may be compared to the north pole star, which keeps its place and all the stars turn towards it.[38]

In this context, one may find it hard to define *li* since its meaning is extensive. Bodde and Morris agree that in the narrowest sense, *li* refers to the proper performance of customary rites and in the broadest sense, *li* dictates harmony as the basis for political and social relationships.[39] Another writer, Hu Hsien-Chin, summarizes the concept of *li* as follows:

> *Li* is best expressed as approved patterns of behaviour between individuals standing in a definite relationship to each other, and in conformance with a definite system of values relating to such definite relationships .. *li* has a coercive power almost as great as law, but transmitted to the individual by the socialization process of childhood and youth, the personality comes to perform its dictates automatically.[40]

Confucianism sought to emphasize upon differentiation. The Five Cardinal Relationships advocated by Confucius were those as between the ruler and the subject, the father and the son, the husband and the wife, the elder brother and the younger brother, and friend and friend. This principle of *li* took into account the existence of a social hierarchy brought about as a result of humanity being born unequal in 'intelligence and virtue'.[41] This led to a distinct division of labour: the mental and the physical. Mencius,[42] a disciple of Confucian thinking, asserted that:

> Great men have their proper business .. some labour with their minds, and some labour with their strength. Those who labour with their minds govern others; those who labour with their strength are governed by others. Those who are governed by others support them; those who govern others are supported by them. This is a principle universally recognised.[43]

In short, in any society, certain differences were bound to exist. What was important was to have one's status clearly defined and one's role properly performed in order to achieve a harmonious living.

The enforcement of *li* was through public opinion, which was very powerful, and was also made possible by the various local organizations which frequently held informal talks with the masses. There was also the common basis of culture insured by the civil service examinations which led to the ethical principles being authoritatively recognized state-wide.[44]

Bodde and Morris have indicated that 'what is uniquely Chinese ... is [the] insistence upon the moral and political dangers involved in the public promulgation of legal norms. This view of law seems to have no real parallel in any other civilization'.[45] This meant that in traditional China, popular customary practices based on social ethics outweighed the role of any formally enacted law. An involvement with the law was generally tabooed - 'to involve someone in a lawsuit was a way of ruining him'.[46] It is little wonder that the Great Sage himself said, 'the thing is we should make it our aim that there not be any lawsuits at all'.[47]

It was apparent that the Confucianists regarded the law as a secondary mediator. The penal nature of the written law (for example, the *Ta Ch'ing Lu Li*) suggested that the law was not meant to be a private remedy but rather, it was 'designed to protect the State from the people, not the people from the State'.[48] It naturally followed that the existence of the courts appeared to provide for the higher administrative levels to adjudicate on cases where the State rights had been infringed upon.

Below is a compilation of some Confucianist contentions against the idea of law:

1.   The Confucian view maintained that humanity was inherently good. Humanity was also possessed of the capability of learning goodness. It was through *li* that a person was cultivated and was thus able to refrain from doing wrong. *Li* was thus preventive, Law (*fa*) was curative and punitive.

2.   In the art of governance, virtue was more desirable than force. *Li* encouraged the cultivation of virtue and sought to promote a virtuous government. Law represented an instrument of a tyrannical government based on compulsion.

3.   *Li* was the product of the intelligent sages of antiquity who were concerned with the principle of harmony. Law was man-made for the purpose of generating political power.

4.   Confucius emphasized the five major relationships - those of emperor and subject, father and son, husband and wife, elder and younger brother, friend and friend - which were regarded as instinctive to humanity and necessary for a stable social order. *Li*

promoted these relationships by laying down rules of behaviour according to status. On the other hand, Law sought to impose an artificial uniformity which ran counter to such instinctive relationships.

5.   *Li* (in terms of rites and ceremony) was artistically inclined. It provided poetry and beauty to life and consequently, a vent for the expression of the necessary human emotions. Law was seen as mechanistic and utilitarian in character.

6.   *Li* was flexible to enable a government to function harmoniously. Law, being more rigidly laid down, enabled people to circumvent it by trickery. This invited the danger of upholding the letter of the Law but not its spirit.

7.   Morality was far more significant than the Law. The rule of a morally-inclined prince was more effective than that of the clever promulgation of any Law.[49]

The Legalist View

Legalism arose out of Chinese politics of the fourth and third centuries B.C.. Its exponents were practising politicians who had little notion of the underlying principles of government but who otherwise recognised the need for more rational organization of society and thus, endeavoured to deal with present problems with direct control methods.[50]

The Legalists adopted the extreme view of government by law alone which was completely antithetical to Confucian thinking. They advocated a system of law and punishment and urged that subjects must be compelled to follow a set of rules. Much stress was laid upon fixed standards as opposed to the Confucian emphasis on personal ethics in government.[51]

Fa, or Law, was defined as 'that which is recorded in the register, set up in the government offices, and promulgated upon the people'.[52] *Fa* seemed to exclude the setting up of virtuous examples by the rulers. It was concerned chiefly with rewards and punishments which were deemed sufficient to secure obedience. Rewards and punishments were the criteria for administration.[53]

A Legalist scholar once remarked:

In ruling the world, one must act in accordance with human nature. In human nature there are the feelings of liking and disliking, and hence rewards and punishments are effective. When rewards and punishments are effective, interdicts and commands can be 'established', and the way of government is complete.[54]

Actions resulting in rewards or punishments were adjudged by 'objective, absolute standards which permitted no differentiation on the basis of personal differences'.[55] Thus, a set of uniform laws to either reward or punish was essential to make everyone obey the authority of the law. Subordination to authority for the building up of the strength of the State was evident and was in direct contrast with the Confucian view that the end of all government was to promote well-being of the subjects and preserve social harmony.

One of the Legalists' theories indicated their distrust of human nature. They claimed that no more than ten persons would do good of their own volition. Thus, it was necessary to have laws to ensure that the people could do no wrong.[56] Without law, there would be much undesirable transgression. Any infringement of right was sought to be remedied by either compensation for the aggrieved or punishment against the wrongdoer.

Ethical norms and moral precepts were of little consequence to the Legalists, or the *Fa chia*, who regarded them as the main concern of the moralists and the educators who could spend time in exerting moral influence. The Legalists maintained that 'a sage ruler relied upon law, not upon wisdom'.[57]

The Legalists sought to capitalize on the inconsistency of human character. They argued that a ruler of high character was rarely found and even so, human nature might not readily respond to the moral examples set down by the ruler. 'A fixed body of law, impartially and firmly administered, will not fluctuate as does the character of princes'.[58]

It was obvious that the Legalists sought to implement laws 'by the most certain processes, the most direct methods, and within the shortest periods of time'.[59] They were primarily interested in power consolidation and the unification of thought through force. History has it that they were instrumental in setting up the dictatorship of the Chin Dynasty (221-206 B.C.), in unifying China in 221 B.C. and in imposing the most stringent control of life and thought in Chinese History.[60]

Although the Legalists succeeded in unifying China in 221 B.C., the supremacy of the Chin Dynasty was shortlived. This period of dynastic rule represented a reign of terror for the Chinese who grew fearful of the ruthlessness of the Legalists and since then have rejected them.

A summary of the Legalists' arguments appears below:

1.   Law was necessary because the great majority of people were motivated by self-interest. Very few were naturally altruistic. Law was concerned with the many selfish persons and not with the few good ones.

2.   Every person was equal before the law. Rank or status was immaterial. The aim of any government was to abolish factionalism and favouritism.

3.   Law could bring about a stable government since it was fixed and known to all. The uniformity of Law contrasted with the flexibility of *li*.

4.   Human societies changed with time. In the ancient days, population was small and life was comparatively simple. But the sharp rise of population growth meant a competitive struggle for existence. One could use the machinery of the Law to organize the people and to impute responsibility to the collectives. Law was, therefore, more suitable because it was able to respond to the needs of changing times. On the other hand, *li* was old-fashioned and static.

5.   The self-interested person could not be sufficiently persuaded to act altruistically. Law imposed rewards or punishments as an effective means to regulate human conduct.

6.   The device of an effective legal machinery would result in the most mediocre ruler being capable of a good administration, provided the laws were abided by.

7.   Harsh laws acted as deterrents. This would, in turn, eradicate the ills of society. The needs of a society would be far better served through the application of laws.[61]

Conclusion

Clearly, the written law in traditional China was a product of political necessity.[62] It was not surprising, therefore, that its emphasis was penal. It was also generally shunned. Unlike Legalism whose measures were remedial, Confucianism was preventive. The popular acceptance of Confucianist moral teaching coupled with the fact that the formal law was rejected as harsh and inhuman during the Chin Dynasty (221-206 B.C.) resulted, to a great extent, in the negative attitude of the Chinese towards Law. Law was considered to be one of the last corrective agencies.

Moreover, the Chinese found the idea of a 'personal divine lawgiver' quite unacceptable.[63] They viewed the need for the formal enactment of laws to be 'indicative of a serious moral decline'.[64]

A survey of the above Schools of legal thinking leads one to the conclusion that Confucianism seemed to be a more favoured course and approach to human governance, seen as a more effective means of maintaining social order and harmonious inter-personal relationships in the traditional Chinese society.

Confucianism was more acceptable in the Chinese traditional society because of the emphasis placed on the cultivation of moral virtue, the promotion of human values and the development of individual personality, social harmony in conformity with the cosmic order, and the overriding stress on education.

But, in order to study the Chinese legal tradition, as has been rightly pointed out by Chu T'ung-tsu, the legal codes must be compared with the books of *li*, lest its 'origin and meaning' could not be grasped.[65] *Li* and *fa*, though separate entities, were complementary to each other in establishing social order. This could be seen in later times when, Mencius, though a Confucian scholar, acknowledged the fact that 'Virtue alone is not sufficient for the exercise of government; Laws alone cannot carry themselves into practice'.[66] This combined theory of a good government led subsequently to the concept of the 'Confucianization of Law'.[67]

It should perhaps be borne in mind that the ultimate aim of both these Schools of Chinese legal thinking was the maintenance of social order via an effective government. Their difference lay in 'what constituted an ideal social order and by what means such an order could be attained'.[68]

The dominant influence of Confucianism in the traditional Chinese way of life has been continually passed down to future generations.[69] This being true, the negative attitude shown towards law is still apparent among the Chinese: some good examples are found in scholastic studies,[70] and my own observations in Malaysia, particularly in the rural areas.

In the absence of law as an effective means of regulating human conduct, in the sense of inter-personal relationships, one must endeavour to discover the non-legal means that have helped in the maintenance of order in traditional Chinese society. This exposition, then, falls into the domain of the succeeding Chapter.

NOTES

1   Confucius, *The Analects*, XII:13.

2   Interview took place on 16 August 1982 at the Lord President's Chambers, Federal Court, Kuala Lumpur.

3   See page 8 of Chapter 1, above.

4   See Goh Bee Chen, 'Culture and Mediation' in Laurence Boulle, *Mediation: Skills and Techniques*, Butterworths, Sydney, 2001, at page 7.

5   Sybille van der Sprenkel, *Legal Institutions in Manchu China: A Sociological Analysis*, University of London The Athlone Press, London, 1962, at page 115.

6   See Simon Roberts, *Order And Dispute: An Introduction To Legal Anthropology*, Penguin Books, Harmondsworth, 1978, at page 23.

7   Dennis Lloyd, *The Idea of Law*, Penguin Books, Harmondsworth, 1977, at page 71. Similarly, Elvin maintains that 'Traditional China, seen from the Western Perspective, lacked a social and intellectual dimension – that of law, justice and jurisprudence'. See Mark Elvin, *Changing Stories in the Chinese World*, Stanford University Press, Stanford, 1997, at page 32.

8   See Goh Bee Chen, *Negotiating With The Chinese*, Dartmouth Publishing Company, Aldershot/Brookfield, 1996, Chapter 3.

9   Kenneth Scott Latourette, *THE CHINESE, Their History And Culture*, Macmillan Company, New York, 1964, at page 45. See also Ralph H. Folsom and John H. Minan (eds), *Law in the People's Republic of China: Commentary, Readings and Materials*, Martinus Nijhoff Publishers, Dordrecht, 1989, at page 86.

10   G. Jamieson, *Chinese Family And Commercial Law*, Vetch and Lee Limited, Hong Kong, 1970, at page i. See also Phillip M. Chen, *Law and Justice: The Legal System in China 2400 B.C. To 1960 A.D.*, Dunellen Publishing Company, New York, 1973, at page 84.

11   Sybille van der Sprenkel, note 5 above, at page 33. See also Stanley B. Lubman and Gregory C. Wajnowski, 'International Commercial

Dispute Resolution In China: A Practical Assessment' (1993) 4 *American Review of International Arbitration* 107, at page 111.

[12] For a comprehensive explanation of *li*, see Chu T'ung -tsu, *Law and Society in Traditional China*, Mouton & Co., Paris/La Haye, 1961, at pages 230-241.

[13] See Derk Bodde and Clarence Morris, *Law in Imperial China*, Harvard University Press, Cambridge (Massachusetts), 1967, at page 11.

[14] Derk Bodde and Clarence Morris, note 13 above, at page 20. See also Geoffrey MacCormack, 'Natural Law and Cosmic Harmony in Traditional Chinese Thought' (1989) 2 *Ratio Juris* 254, who asserts that there are subtle distinctions in the Western and Chinese conceptions of 'natural law', at pages 254-257. For a more detailed discussion of the Chinese cosmological worldview, see Geoffrey MacCormack, *The Spirit of Traditional Chinese Law*, The University of Georgia Press, Athens & London, 1996.

[15] William H. McNeill and Jean W. Sedlar (eds), *Classical China*, Oxford University Press, New York, 1960, at page 76.

[16] Derk Bodde and Clarence Morris, note 13 above, at page 3.

[17] Sybille van der Sprenkel, note 5 above, at page 1.

[18] Phillip M. Chen, note 10 above, at page 84.

[19] Charles Sumner Lobingier, 'An Introduction to Chinese Law', *China Law Review*, vol. 4, at page 121.

[20] Stanley Lubman, 'Mao and Mediation: Politics and Dispute Resolution in Communist China', (1967) 55 *California Law Review*, at page 1295. Lubman gives a good historical introduction concerning traditional Chinese dispute settlement method leading up to the Communist Period.

[21] Phillip M. Chen, note 10 above, at pages 7-9.

[22] Chu T'ung-tsu, note 12 above, at page 284.

[23] Chu T'ung-tsu, note 12 above, at page 9; Derk Bodde and Clarence Morris, note 13 above, at pages 17 and 50.

[24] Phillip M. Chen, note 10 above, at page 8.

[25] Wm. Theodore de Barry, Chan Wing-tsit and Burton Watson (compl.), *Sources of Chinese Tradition*, Columbia University Press, New York/London, 1966, at page 17.

[26] Wm. Theodore de Barry, Chan Wing-tsit and Burton Watson (comp.), note 25 above, at page 17.

[27] It is not known whether these dates could be in error by a few years. See Kenneth S. Latourette, note 9 above, at page 54.

[28] A Confucian saying translated by Lin Yu-tang, *The Wisdom of Confucius*, (1938) at page 241, quoted in John M. Koller, *Oriental Philosophies*, Charles Scribner's Sons, New York, 1970, at page 223.

[29] *The Analects*, XVII:2. See Wu Teh Yao, *Politics East-Politics West*, Pan Pacific Book Distributors Ltd., Singapore, 1979, at page 115.

30   *Ta-Tai Li Chi*, 2, 16 in Chu T'ung-tsu, note 12 above, at page 249.

31   *Ta-Tai Li Chi*, 2, 16 in Chu T'ung-tsu, note 12 above, at page 249.

32   Soothill (1941), at pages 8-9, quoted in Sybille van der Sprenkel, note 5 above, at page 30. See also Legge, *Chinese Classics*, I, 9, in Chu T'ung-tsu, note 12 above, at page 251.

33   Lu Chia (third and second centuries B.C.).

34   Huan Kuan, *Yen t'ieh lun*, 10, 6b-7a, in Chu T'ung-tsu, note 1 above, at page 248.

35   John M. Koller, note 18 above, at page 214.

36   *The Book of Yu*, III, 5, in Wu Teh Yao, note 29 above, at page 77.

37   Chu T'ung-tsu, note 12 above, at page 240.

38   *The Analects*, II:1. See also Wu Teh Yao, note 29 above, at page 189.

39   Derk Bodde and Clarence Morris, note 13 above, at page 19.

40   Hu Hsien-Chin (1948), at page 53, quoted in Sybille van der Sprenkel, note 5 above, at page 31.

41   Chu T'ung-tsu, note 12 above, at page 226.

42   Mencius (371-289 B.C.). One of his contributions being that government should be by good example of the rulers, and not by force. He maintained that people were by nature good and must be educated in an environment made favourable by good will, music and art. See Kenneth S. Latourette, note 9 above, at page 55.

43   Mencius, 5B, 16-2a; Legge, note 32 above, at pages 125-126, quoted in Chu T'ung-tsu, note 12 above, at page 226.

44   Kenneth S. Latourette, note 9 above, at page 467.

45   Derk Bodde and Clarence Morris, note 13 above, at page 17.

46   Sybille van der Sprenkel, note 5 above, at page 123.

47   *The Analects*, XII: 13. John M. Koller, note 28 above, at page 219.

48   Phillip M. Chen, note 10 above, at page 10.

49   Derk Bodde and Clarence Morris, note 13 above at pages 20-21.

50   de Barry, Chan and Watson (compl), note 25 above, at page 136.

51   McNeill and Sedlar (ed), note 15 above, at page 75.

52   Fung Yu-Lan (1968) at page 162 quoted in Sybille van der Sprenkel, note 5 above, at page 33.

53   Chu T'ung-tsu, note 12 above, at page 241; Wu Teh Yao, note 29 above, at page 187.

54   Quoted in Han Fei-tzu (233 B.C.), Fung, note 52 above, at page 162. This view comes close to that of the English analytical jurist, Bentham (1748-1832), who asserted that the business of government was to promote the happiness of society by furthering the enjoyment of pleasure and affording security against pain in his utilitarian approach towards law. See Edgar Bodenheimer, *Jurisprudence - the Philosophy and Method of the Law*, Harvard University Press, Cambridge/Massachusetts, 1967, at pages 82-85.

55   Phillip M. Chen, note 10 above, at page 30.

[56]   Fung (1948), note 52 above, at page 160, in Sybille van der Sprenkel, note 5 above, at page 32.

[57]   *Kuan-tzu*, 15:4a, in Chu T'ung-tsu, note 12 above, at page 260.

[58]   K.S. Latourette, note 9 above, at page 59.

[59]   Chu T'ung-tsu, note 12 above, at page 261.

[60]   Chan Wing-tsit (trans), *A Sourcebook in Chinese Philosophies*, Princeton University Press, New Jersey, 1963, at page 251.

[61]   Derk Bodde and Clarence Morris, note 13 above, at pages 23-24.

[62]   Derk Bodde and Clarence Morris, note 13 above, at pages 48-49.

[63]   Dennis Lloyd, note 7 above, at page 71. Also, Derk Bodde and Clarence Morris, note 13 above, at page 10.

[64]   Derk Bodde and Clarence Morris, note 13 above, at page 49.

[65]   Chu T'ung-tsu, note 12 above, at page 278.

[66]   *The Works of Mencius*, Book 4 Part 1 Paragraph 3, in Wu Teh Yao, note 29 above, at pages 138 and 191.

[67]   For details, see Chu T'ung-tsu, note 12 above, at pages 267-279.

[68]   Chu T'ung-tsu, note 12 above, at page 226.

[69]   See Hu Chang-tu, *China-Its People, Its Society, Its Culture*, Hraf Press, New Haven, 1960, at page 11: 'The Chinese people ... love to read and retell the past, which to many is a mirror reflecting the present'.

[70]   See, for instance, Michael J. Moser, *Law And Social Change In A Chinese Community: A Case Study From Rural Taiwan*, Oceana Publications Inc, London, 1982; Madeleine Zelin, 'Merchant Dispute Mediation in Twentieth-Century Zigong, Sichuan' in Kathryn Bernhardt and Philip C.C. Huang, *Civil Law in Qing and Republican China*, Stanford University Press, Stanford, 1994, at pages 249-286; Jerold S. Auerbach, *Justice Without Law?*, Oxford University Press, New York, 1983, at pages 73-76.

3   Social Sanctions as a Force of Law

First follow your personal sentiment, then follow the dictates of reason, then follow the law.[1]

Introduction

At this juncture, it may be interesting to pause for a moment to reflect upon the essentially non-litigious character of Chinese society. This is particularly relevant in view of the fact that in Chapter 2, we explored the idea of the secondary role the Law plays for the traditional Chinese in general. In Western jurisprudence, Law is regarded with supremacy and respect. Similarly, legal institutions and the machinery employed in the implementation of laws and rules are almost regarded as sacrosanct. On the other hand, the Chinese position contrasts sharply with such an observation. Something else then must fill this void and produce a desirable and orderly society for the Chinese in a similar fashion. My proposition is that customary norms and social precepts quite happily satisfy such a social requirement for order and stability, and, in the case of the Chinese, the paramountcy of harmony. I have, in fact, come to regard these Chinese customary norms and social precepts as attaining a status the equivalent of Western juridical aspirations. They are not only practically relevant, but enjoy an informal 'legal' relationship with its participants in the sense that they compel social obedience the way that promulgated laws and regulations in the West are seen to be doing.

To reiterate, traditional Chinese society can be said to have been a non-legally oriented one. The following illustration bears testimony to this observation:

We Chinese don't like to go to court... Unlike you foreigners, we have 5,000 years of civilization behind us. And our great traditions have taught us too that the correct way to settle our differences is to yield to each other, like brothers living in the same house. The only people who would bring a suit in court are those who don't care about their face. But people of this kind are unreasonable, and luckily rare.[2]

This, according to old Chinese thinking, may be attributed to the fact that humanity and nature formed an 'unbroken continuum' such that social disorder was reflected in an undue disturbance of the total cosmic order.[3] Hence, the Confucian insistence on the performance of proper ritual and correct ceremony in conformity with *li*. Only in this way could humanity live in peace and harmony. Once again, we experience the pervasiveness of Confucian thought in the day-to-day life and conduct of the average Chinese.

Jamieson notes that Chinese legislation did not differentiate the civil from the criminal. Both types of proceedings appeared to warrant penalties when guilt was established.[4] One recalls from the foregoing Chapter that ancient Chinese written law was essentially penal in emphasis. And, as Bodde and Morris point out, 'the official law always operated in a vertical direction from the State upon the individual, rather than on a horizontal plane directly between two individuals'.[5] This naturally meant and resulted in the fact that matters of a civil nature were largely left to individual self-help. In this connection, with regard to conflicts and their resolution, Lubman observes that in traditional China, Confucian ideology interacted with existing social institutions to produce a desirable 'mediational style of dispute settlement'.[6]

As is commonly observed, traditional Chinese society had as its basic unit not the individual but the various groups and social units to which he or she belonged. The most basic of these units is the family. Moreover, traditional Chinese society was known to consist of large kin groups which represented an extension of the family concept.[7] Relations amongst these groups were often amicable. Direct confrontation in the event of a dispute was tactfully avoided to preserve inter-personal harmony and relationships. To this end, reconciliation was preferred.[8]

Therefore, what in the Western legal tradition was called the civil law was in China to be found in the prevailing rules of customary behaviour in the family which could be instanced in the

Chinese law of succession and inheritance and the marriage law.[9]
Since early times, Chinese social sanctions have differed from legal sanctions in that the former originate from *li* -i.e. the tenets of Confucian teaching - while the latter trace their origin to the Legalist School.[10] In this respect, the traditional Chinese social sanctions have to be examined. Their effective observance has been partly responsible for the negative attitude of the Chinese in general towards the Law and the Courts. One explanation is that these social sanctions possess 'a coercive power almost as great as law',[11] and they help to regulate the ordinary affairs of lay people.

Before I deliberate upon the Chinese social sanctions, it is a relevant point to highlight the concept of family since it played a significant role in enforcing and perpetuating such social sanctions in the traditional Chinese society.

The Concept of Family in Traditional Chinese Life

As mentioned earlier, of all the social units in traditional Chinese life, the family, or *chia*, was the most basic. It was also patriarchal.[12] In this connection, one notes that of the Five Cardinal Relationships in Confucian *li*, i.e. those of emperor and subject, father and son, husband and wife, older brother and younger brother, and friend and friend, three arise within the conception of the family. These relationships are, importantly, recognized as being hierarchical in nature. Thus, in Confucianism, the family is the foundation of the larger social and political order.[13] In the old days, it was believed that if the family units were stable and ordered, all would be well for the state.

In the traditional view, the father was the head of the family authority. He was known as the *chia chang*, or the senior male of the family.[14] However, in a family comprising three generations, the grandfather represented the supreme authority.[15] On the demise of the father or when the father became incapacitated due to illness, the son[16] assumed the position as the family head. In extraordinary cases, a widow of strong character might act as the head of the family.[17]

The *chia chang* was the family provider. His family responsibilities were great: he had to oversee the economic well-being of his family members, maintain order and discipline within the family, ensure a good family reputation and tolerate no violation of the existing social norms by any of the family members, and perform the ancestral rites in reverence of the ancestors' spirits.[18] In this way, one can see that in the traditional Chinese family, the *chia chang* was seen to perform several important economic and social roles not only within the family unit but extending to the social circle as well. The implication was that his authority came to be regarded no less regulatory than merely social. His command was the law, so to speak. It is in this light that it is made easier to understand why the Chinese are a generally socially cohesive group and why they are more inclined to look towards customary norms, a product of their social organization, as attaining the equivalent status of Western legal norms.

Another important feature related to the Chinese conception of property and inheritance and succession matters. Traditionally, all the family property vested in the father at his sole disposal.[19] No child could own property in his own right during the father's lifetime. Any violation of this rule was considered unfilial.[20] At the death of the father, the son succeeded him and the same principles applied from generation to generation. This basically formed the Chinese law of succession and inheritance. It was a Confucian tenet reduced to a customary practice passed down since time immemorial and, being custom, everyone was presumed to know of its existence.[21] There was, therefore, no difficulty in applying this 'law' since it was understood to be the traditional way of doing things.

Since only the son could succeed to the family property, perpetuate the family lineage and perform ancestral worship, it was of fundamental importance for the traditional Chinese man to have a male offspring. Thus, sons were 'desired intensely' and were regarded more important than the daughters.[22] Mencius was quoted as saying, 'there are three things which are unfilial and to have no posterity is the greatest of them'.[23] Here, 'posterity' meant a male offspring. In our modern, contemporary context, it may be noted, the requirement for a male offspring is seen as desirable rather than mandatory.

In the traditional sense, because of the insistence on a male heir, the meaning of marriage differed from the Western outlook. Under the Common Law Justice system, the decisions from early case-law suggested that the purpose of marriage was for companionship. The matrimonial union was a voluntary one entered into between a man and a woman.[24] In contrast, for the Chinese, 'ancestor worship was ... the first and the last purpose of marriage'.[25] This difference relating to the law of marriage between the Common Law and Chinese customary law consequently gave rise to wider implications. For instance, a common law marriage was monogamous and a Chinese marriage was 'monogamous' subject to the right of concubinage.[26]

The Confucian text explains the meaning of marriage to be 'a bond of affection between two surnames. It serves the ancestral temple on the one hand and continues the family line on the other'.[27] As such, in contrast with the West, marriage became the concern of the family rather than the individual.[28]

In the family context, it was important for the spirits of the ancestors to be sacrificed to. Otherwise, they became 'unworshipped ghosts'.[29] In fact, the Confucian ethical discipline traditionally demanded a great deal of the observances of ritualistic practices. Strictly speaking, good propriety included carrying out religiously the duties of ancestral worship. In this connection, since the male heir alone was qualified to perform ancestral worship, an unmarried man or a father without a son was considered unfilial: 'just as one has a duty to render piety to one's ancestors, so one must, for their sake, see to it that one leaves a successor behind to venerate their memory'.[30] This factor has accounted largely for the Chinese cultural desire for a male offspring, and reiterates the role a male plays in the family and social environments.

It naturally followed that there was a moral obligation resting on the traditional Chinese man to marry for the purpose of producing a male offspring to continue ancestral worship.[31] A childless father or a father without any male offspring was compelled to adopt one,[32] or to take in a concubine.[33]

The true object of taking in a concubine was to beget a son to perpetuate the husband's family lineage. In traditional China, a *chieh*, meaning concubine, literally implied 'an established girl' giving her a proper status in the family.[34] Normally, she was taken in after having obtained permission from the wife. Her position was, therefore, inferior to that of the wife and she 'enjoyed no comparable rights'.[35] This essential distinction ought to be grasped for one to effectively comprehend the Chinese Family Law, particularly the law relating to marriage.[36]

In the traditional Confucian view, the position of the wife was subordinated to that of the husband.[37] It was said that 'the husband's authority replaced the father's'.[38] An interesting observation made regarding the Mandarin character *fu*, meaning 'woman', is that it is a combination of 'female' and 'broom' which bears the meaning of 'to serve' and 'to submit'.[39] This again explains the rule by the *chia chang* and illustrates the principle of 'no two authorities in one family'.[40]

The inferior position assumed by the female in the traditional Chinese society formed part of Confucian *li*. Preservation of family order was only possible when there was only one voice to be heard in the family - and that voice was to come from the senior male. It may be noted that this feature essentially illustrates the hierarchical nature of Confucian tenets, as alluded to earlier.[41] In this respect, one may well argue that such a disadvantageous position was grossly unfair to the Chinese female. Yet, one has also to acknowledge the fact that it has survived the time-tested Chinese social order to give rise to family solidarity and social harmony.

It has often been said that the relationship between the father and the son provided the basis for the exercise of authority in traditional China.[42] In theory at least, the father held the power of life and death over his offspring.[43] On the one hand, the traditional idea insisted upon the son's absolute submission to the authority of the father and imposed a duty on the son to respect and support his parents in their old age. On the other hand, it was the responsibility of the father to support his son and provide a wife for him. The relationship between the father and son was, therefore, seen in this closely-intertwined economic and social position.[44] Such a relationship also testified to the principle of reciprocity within Confucianism. The legal implication arrived at from such a relationship was that matters relating to succession and inheritance and marriage were regulated by the family.

The mother's relationship vis-a-vis the son was based more on affection than on authority. In the traditional view, a mother's status in the family was elevated when she gave birth to a male offspring. Prior to the son's arrival, her position in the family was 'unenviable'.[45] This was consonant with the view that the purpose of marriage was to obtain a male heir who could then continue ancestral worship. It is in this sense that a Chinese notion of marriage is more functional than romantic, when compared with the Westerner's.

The relationship between both parents and the daughter was 'less formally defined'.[46] The old view was that the daughter was only a 'temporary member' who was the responsibility of the family up to the time of her marriage.[47] In fact, upon her marriage, her birth family would come to be referred to as 'the outside family', indicating a somewhat severance of a relationship with her own parents.

In the Chinese view, the proper regulation of the State must be preceded by the proper regulation of the respective families concerned.[48] It was thought that the family constituted the foundation of the social order and consequently, a collection of good families would produce a stable and orderly society, and, by extension, a stable and well-ordered country. As such, relationships within the family were given particular stress. It must again be remembered and reinforced that 'of the five relations emphasized by the traditional moral standards and reinforced by Confucianism - those between prince and minister, father and son, older brother and younger brother, husband and wife, and friend and friend - three were in the family.'[49] This again demonstrates the significance of the family in traditional Chinese life.

The obligations of a child in the family were succinctly stated by van der Sprenkel:

> One owed respect, obedience and support to family superiors during their lifetime and veneration with prescribed ritual and within prescribed degrees after death. From these obligations there arose other derived obligations: to value one's body as a gift from one's forebears, to add lustre to the family name, to continue the line of descent and to acquire the means to provide fittingly for the departed.[50]

One is reminded of the fact that the concept of family in the traditional Chinese sense actually comprised larger kin groups. This is unlike the Western conception of the family which is essentially referable to the nuclear family. For the Chinese, kinsmen could be identified through parental relations, or through marriage. Another type of kindred was the patrilineal clan, or *tsu*, which was 'a common descent group tracing its ancestry to a first male ancestor who settled in a given locality'.[51] The *tsu* was said to consist of many families bearing a common surname. On the supposition that all the members within the *tsu* originally came from one large family, endogamous marriages were prohibited.[52] This prohibitory rule has formed a strong sanction to this day.[53]

Based on the foregoing, it can scarcely be denied that the traditional Chinese society was family-centred.[54] The family and the clan dominated the individual. As a Chinese proverb goes: 'The family has its own law, the lineage its own regulations'.[55] Thus, an individual's behaviour was conditioned by his family and clan rules and his actions checked by means of certain existing norms of society. Most of the existing social norms were a result of some 'family' rules. The sanction underlying the breach was social ostracism, which was very powerful.[56]

Thus, what follows will be a discussion of some of the family rules existing in the traditional Chinese society before the social sanctions proceed to be highlighted upon.

Family Rules

In traditional Chinese life, Confucian virtues played a significant role in establishing certain family rules. Koller, too, attempts to explain the fact that the word '*li*' - the key term in Confucianism - has a wide meaning.[57] One of the meanings includes 'a system of well-defined social relationships with definite attitudes towards one another, love in the parents, filial piety in the children, respect in the younger brothers, friendliness in the elder brothers, loyalty among friends, respect for authority among subjects and benevolence in rulers'.[58] Of all these emphases, the corner-stone of the old Chinese family system was the Confucian virtue of *hsiao*, commonly interpreted as filial piety.[59]

Confucius himself defined *hsiao* to be: 'that parents, when alive, should be served according to propriety; that, when dead, they should be buried according to propriety, and that they should be sacrificed to according to propriety'.[60] This, in the traditional view, lay in the acceptance that life itself originated from the parents and as such, one should not act in any way as to cause physical harm to the body,[61] nor should one by any misconduct tarnish the family name. One was encouraged to do well in life by becoming economically wealthy or scoring high marks in the scholastic examinations so as to make the parents' (and thus, the family) name well-known and respected. Thus, the virtue of *hsiao* demanded physical, emotional and spiritual fulfilment.[62] Above all, it embodied the requirement of reverence. Once when asked by a student on the subject of filial piety, Confucius replied: 'Nowadays a filial son is just a man who keeps his parents in food. But even dogs or horses are given food. If there is no feeling of reverence, wherein lies the difference?'[63]

As a necessary corollary, central to the virtue of *hsiao* was respect for superior authority. In this connection, Lee Yan Phou states:

The child is early taught to walk respectfully behind his superiors, to sit only when he is bidden, to speak only when questions are asked him, and to salute his superiors by the correct designations. It would be the height of impropriety for him to mention his father's name, or call his uncle and elder brothers by their names... [He] must rise from his seat when any relatives approach him. If he is taken to task for anything he has done he must never contradict, never seek to explain. The Chinese take no explanations from those subject to them. They deem this method absolutely necessary for the preservation of authority.[64]

It was generally believed that when the child learnt the virtue of reverence for his own parents and superiors, the same virtue would also influence his actions outside of the family. *Hsiao,* though a family virtue having its foundation in the family, could be extended to become 'a moral and social virtue', i.e. the child would ultimately learn universal respect and love.[65] Once this was achieved, his actions would spring from a humane basis.

Such a humane basis was called *jen*, or benevolence, human-heartedness. It had its root in *hsiao*. Koller regards it as the buttressing factor in the Golden Rule of Confucius, i.e. the idea that 'Man is the measure of Man'.[66] The oft-cited Confucian tenet of 'do not do unto others what you would not others do unto you' represents a constituent part of this concept of *jen*.

It has been pointed out by Koller that the three most important concepts contained in the Confucian *li* are *hsiao, jen* and *yi*. All of them were associated with the concept of family in the traditional Chinese life. *Yi*, or righteousness, properly cultivated in a person, enabled him to be morally-inclined. One acted according to *yi* absolutely and unconditionally for the pure reason that such actions were considered right. For example, 'a person ought to respect and obey his parents because it is morally right and obligatory to do so, and for no other reason'.[67] What was, therefore, important was to be possessed of a moral sense to recognize good and bad, and to distinguish right from wrong.

The above Confucian virtues were sought to be properly instilled and constituted in the traditional Chinese family. One must remember the fact that, in the Confucian view, the State was made up of many families and if each family was well-regulated, it would certainly augur well for the harmony and stability within the State. To quote Koller again: 'if, without enforced positive law (in the relevant sense), there is to be peace and well-being, it is necessary that everyone act appropriately, or practise the virtue of *li*. To act appropriately one must respect and care for others, or practise the virtue of *jen*, and this respect for men is learned early through respect for the parents, or by practising the virtue of *hsiao*'.[68] Once again, this highlights the importance of these family rules.

It was also vital for the continued practice of these family rules that they be constantly enforced and widely publicized. To this end, informal lectures on Confucian ethical principles 'to indoctrinate the illiterate masses' were frequently held at compulsory meetings called 'village pacts', i.e. gatherings of the common people.[69]

To reiterate, the virtue of *hsiao* constituted the first commandment and precept of the family.[70] From this principal virtue, other virtues and obligations were derived.[71]

Social Sanctions

It is, first of all, necessary to grasp the meaning of social sanctions. Generally speaking, in any society, certain norms of behaviour are considered necessary to allow the members of that society to assume some fundamental politeness in their dealings with one another. They also help to keep society moving pleasantly and with the minimum of friction. Quite commonly, the fear of shame, the concern for 'what others think', the sensitivity to ridicule or criticism, and the threat of exposure to disgust appear to provide effective social control mechanisms. In this connection, Simon Roberts contends that personal action is principally motivated by 'how other people will react', and that public reprobation may entail 'ridicule, loss of prestige, physical retaliation, appeal to third parties for some kind of intervention, resort to sorcery, the withdrawal of valued cooperation, or even total ostracism'.[72] All these negative effects constitute strong prohibitions. For instance, in a study of a rural Taiwanese community, Moser made the following pertinent observation:

> Among the sanctions which were employed to enforce conformity to social norms the most severe was the threat of withdrawal of community support to disputants, or social ostracism.[73]

Another writer, Epstein, maintains that the sense of shame may be regarded as a universal force in all social control systems, albeit different societies attach different weight to it.[74] What is fundamental to the understanding of social sanctions is the fact that they are effective 'through the desire of the individual to obtain the approbation and to avoid the disapprobation of his fellows, to win such rewards and to avoid such punishment as the community offers or threatens'.[75] In other words, social sanctions are enforced principally through public opinion. They differ from legal sanctions in the sense that the enforcement of the latter is backed by the authority of the law. Yet, the power of social sanctions cannot be under-estimated. This is chiefly because they are seen as a natural product of one's socialization, and further, their common application often entails one's unconscious subjection. Peer group pressure is easily a compelling force in securing obedience.

Considered within the purview of the traditional Chinese society, it is hardly surprising that in the absence of an inclination towards recourse to the formal law, various social sanctions have evolved and developed to help regulate the ordinary affairs and to maintain peace and order within the society. We have seen in the last Chapter that Chinese social sanctions have been known to originate from Confucian *li*. Though lacking in legal authority, they were upheld by the strong force of social approval or disapproval. Public censure and social ostracism came to be regarded as much-feared punishments.[76]

Some of these social rules of behaviour began as family rules, which have already been deliberated upon. What remains to be discussed are the other types of social sanctions which represent a strong and valid force, to wit, the principle of 'face', the value of *ganqing* or good relations, the precepts of *guanxi* or personal relations and *renqing* or personal goodwill . In this connection, it is particularly relevant to recall the traditioanl Chinese proverb of '*heqing, heli, hefa*', i.e. 'first follow your personal sentiment, then follow the dictates of reason, then follow the law'.

Face

'The Chinese have an obsession with the concept of face, which operates as a powerful social sanction'.[77] The principle of 'face' is the Chinese equivalent of 'honour'.[78] 'Face' is construed to mean 'one's accumulated moral and social prestige in the eyes of the community'.[79] Traditionally, it constituted a powerful factor in enforcing certain existing rules of behaviour by securing conformity to social norms. Van der Sprenkel refers to the principle of 'face' as 'a constant concern to stand well in the opinions of others and in one's own opinion of oneself [because] the business of life was easier for those who kept the respect of their neighbours and their own self-respect'.[80] Hence, the significance of this cultural value in the traditional Chinese life. In this regard, Latourette, too, has perceptively pointed out that the considerations of 'face' played a far greater role in ancient China than in some other countries.[81] Further, in the words of Pye:

> The heavy use of shame as a social control mechanism from the time of early childhood tends to cause feelings of dependency and anxieties about self-esteem, which naturally produces self-consciousness about most social relationships. As a result, a great deal can be gained by helping the Chinese to win face and a great deal will be lost by any affront or slight, no matter how unintended.[82]

The analysis of the concept of face-saving is different culturally for the Chinese and the Westerners. In the case of the Chinese, face-saving is dictated by two aspects: one is self-related, and the other is other-related. This means to say that a Chinese person normally goes to great lengths to prevent a dispute from arising or to try to resolve a problem in order to save the face of the other party as well as his own. But, his actions are, first and foremost, primarily motivated by considerations of the other person. In the latter case, a Westerner is more likely to think about saving her own face and care little for the face of the other person. Such a characteristic is seen as an incident of individualism. Therefore, though we may be thinking about face-saving behaviour in human relationships, its implications and meanings do differ in cultural respect for the Chinese and the Westerner.

The fear of losing face is a good enough reason for the Chinese preoccupation with the prevention of disputes. If an occasion arises which faintly hints at the souring of relationships, the Chinese party will normally tend to perceive this as an event antecedent to a dispute, and will try her hardest to smoothen any ill feelings and restore harmony. Disputing is regarded as discordant and disharmonious, highly disagreeable with the collectivist Chinese nature as well as ethically repugnant to the Confucian

Chinese. The face sanction may, therefore, be said to persist from ancient times to the present.

Interestingly, it may be noted that for the Chinese, the principle of 'face' actually comprises two related conceptions, viz. *mien-tze* and *lien*. Yan refers to the former as 'social' and the latter as 'moral'.[83] Both conceptions refer to the physical face but differ in their metaphorical connotations: *mien-tze* amounts to 'prestige and reputation' which could be added or subtracted while *lien* means 'good character and personal integrity', to be preserved intact or forfeited.[84] It is, in truth, the moral aspect that we are concerned with in the preservation of social harmony and minimization of conflicts.

In securing obedience, *lien* plays a more important part. For instance, the phrase, *pu yao lien* - 'to forfeit face' – has been traditionally regarded as a strong sanction.[85] As Hu Hsien-Chin puts it, the fear of losing *lien* 'keeps up consciousness of moral boundaries, maintains moral values, and expresses the force of social sanctions'.[86] It may be remarked that when conflicts are out in the open, 'it is usually the person in a superior social position who is more vulnerable to sanction by public opinion'.[87] This is attributable to the fact that a person who enjoys a higher social standing is required to maintain more dignity, and hence, more susceptible to social scrutiny.[88]

In this regard, Kirkbride and Tang succinctly describe the precept of face in the following manner:

> A person is socially condemned if he has no *lien* and is seen to be unsuccessful and low in status if he has no *mien-tze*. They are externally mediated and people interact with a purpose to add, give, take, compete, exchange or borrow 'face'.[89]

In a similar vein, Yan insightfully observes, 'The concern with face, especially moral face, provides an internal moral constraint that directs individuals' actions...[and] in real life one's concern with moral face can hardly be separated from the fear of external social sanctions'.[90] It can, therefore, be seen that the principle of 'face' has operated as a strong social control mechanism in the traditional Chinese society still today.[91]

Ganqing

Another valid social principle passed down from time immemorial is the value of *ganqing*, 'good relations', a principle which still holds true today. Van der Sprenkel calls it 'a warm personal relationship between two otherwise unrelated individuals of unequal status'.[92] In the old days, it was considered beneficial to establish *ganqing* with as many people as possible since mutual regard necessitated the granting of favours. *Ganqing* is also related to 'face' in the sense that pressure could be exerted to obtain a favour by invoking *ganqing* and the failure to grant the favour would make the party seeking the favour lose 'face'.[93] As such, *ganqing* has been seen as a valued principle of social intercourse and bears a direct relationship with the principle of face.

Lubman observes that 'personal relationships formed a tightly woven web';[94] more often than not, it was this 'web' that gave rise to *ganqing* and its consequential obligations.

Commonly, *ganqing* is practised in the following manner: it is invoked at the very outset of an impending dispute, or, when the dispute is a matter before the mediator, the mediator would request the disputants to dismiss the dispute and come to some amicable terms with one another on the basis of his *ganqing* with both of them. To take no heed of the mediator's request would amount to disparaging his 'face'. Such is the peculiar working relationship between *ganqing* and *'face'*.[95] And, both these social phenomena have become widely-accepted rules, practised and passed down from generation to generation, finally entrenched within the traditional Chinese way of life. It is no small measure to see its continued practice in modern life.

Guanxi or Personal Relations

Another social precept intertwined with 'face' and *ganqing* is *guanxi* or personal relations. It can also mean 'relationship' or 'connection'.[96] 'It can be described as a special relationship individuals have with each other in which each can make unlimited demands on the other'.[97] *Guanxi* can play a significant role in the settlement of disputes because the stronger the communal relationship is between the two disputing parties, the more obligatory it is for these parties to settle their differences in an amicable way. The dispute is de-personalized, and assumes a communal dimension. All at once, everyone within the community appears to be involved in some small way.

Guanxi can operate in a preventative or remedial way. In the former, the strong bond can help to act to dissipate a dispute. Whenever the parties concerned feel that some major difference is about to arise between them, they are more ready to employ some subtle means to solve the problem themselves. Otherwise, if the situation gets out of control, the dispute will cause them to lose 'face' and it may also mean a loss of face for the community concerned. Furthermore, parties with strong *guanxi* can invoke the *ganqing* between them in order to settle their differences.

In a remedial way, *guanxi* will often be the prime factor that the community calls upon to settle a dispute between the two parties. The community elders will tend to urge the disputants to let bygones be bygones and build up on the good *guanxi* between them. In a society like the Chinese whose focus is on reciprocity and interdependence, *guanxi* is not only theoretically sound but practically viable as well.

Guanxi can again be seen as an effective social control mechanism for the collectivist Chinese. It can operate as a strong social sanction for failure of its observance can entail consequences that go beyond community displeasure.

Renqing or Personal Goodwill

Renqing is 'a peculiarly Chinese characteristic, something Westerners especially sorely lack'.[98] As a concept, it is likened to asking someone to perform favours.[99] The difference is that, in the context of Chinese *renqing*, one is left without a choice. Depending on the degree of the relationship between the parties concerned, it may entail an element of involuntariness.[100] The closer the relationship, the higher the expectation of fulfilling one's *renqing* with the other. One finds one in a position of obligation to render the favour asked of one. This is made possible because '*renqing* means having concern for the face and feelings of one's fellow, and enjoying communality'.[101] One's social success is sometimes measured by the *renqingwei* one maintains with his or her fellow humans. By way of contrast, Westerners normally perform a favour when they consider it convenient to do so and are not put out. The Chinese do not appear to enjoy such a liberty. In fact, the closer the relationship, the more obligatory it is for the favour asked to be carried out.

'In practice, *renqing* represents socially accepted, correct interpersonal behaviour, and the violation of *renqing* is regarded as serious misconduct'.[102] *Renqing*, in this sense, is much like the above social precepts of 'face', *ganqing* and *guanxi*, which are cumulatively the attendant features of friendship or relationship. As Moser puts it:

> In the process of mediating a dispute, it is important for third parties to establish a *renqing* atmosphere so as to terminate the bitterness and quarrelling and lay the groundwork for a settlement.[103]

In a society which constantly strives to achieve and maintain social harmony for its members, it should come across as little surprising that such informal social rules exist to regulate their behaviour. Furthermore, it is interesting to note that these social rules wield such a powerful and compelling force almost comparable to that of law.

Rang or Yielding

Another relevant social value is the notion of *rang* or yielding.[104] This is based on the fact that the attainment of communal peace and harmony can only be made possible through the parties' willingness to compromise, and meet each other mid-way. In this sense, it is not the pursuit of individual rights or justice, but, rather, the restoration of social harmony that represents the desired result should a conflict arise. The Chinese cultural desire for yielding is the prime motivating factor behind the need for compromises, which, in turn, shape the process of any mediation.

In a dispute, a party's pre-disposition to yielding earns her a great deal of respect in the eyes of the community. This is because such a behaviour exhibits good moral upbringing, and is a highly regarded Confucian virtue. Yielding suggests that one has the ability to look within oneself and acknowledge that one may not be completely faultless. After all, it takes two hands to clap. It is also socially expected that the higher the social rank one occupies, the more he is morally obliged to *rang*. A 'superior' person must always set a moral example in the community. If he is seen to concede, his moral standing within the community increases. The 'inferior' person, in turn, feels that his 'face' is being saved, and is more likely to settle the dispute in a peaceable manner.

The virtue of *rang* is closely associated with the observance of Confucian *li*. Sociologically, it is a useful mediation tool in the sense that the process of disputing again incorporates the social dimension and enables the parties concerned to deflect the conflict away from themselves personally and to dissipate it for the communal good.[105]

Conclusion

The social sanctions together with the family rules discussed above can rightly be considered as forming a dominant part of the Chinese traditional cultural heritage. Through their effective observance, the cardinal principle of harmony has been religiously upheld by the traditional Chinese community at large.

Although the traditional concept of the family incorporating the large kin groups in the typical Chinese sense may appear to be wanting to a certain degree in a given society, the rural folk living in a village community are in frequent contact with one another. There is, therefore, a delicate network of inter-personal relationships viewed in a similar context to that of the large kin groups of traditional China. In this respect, Moser's study of the rural Taiwanese,[106] Yan's study of a Chinese village[107] and my own observations in two rural Chinese Malaysian communities[108] support these findings. Furthermore, in the Malaysian context, when the migrant Chinese first settled in the Malay Peninsula, they kept largely to themselves and maintained their own cultural lifestyle. No effort was made to integrate them with the other races.[109] Consequently, they formed close links of fraternity amongst themselves. In order for them to maintain good relations thereby reducing social friction due to such frequent contacts, some commonly accepted or acceptable rules of behaviour or social norms come into play. They are, in fact, mainly the same family rules and social sanctions as discussed above. These customary rules of behaviour and the underlying sanctions are deemed to be vital in the preservation of harmonious relationships with one another. They have been passed down by continued customary practices, by word of mouth, or through Chinese education.[110] Chinese education means imparting the traditional Chinese cultural values and this, in turn, also means that Confucian teachings are revived for the

Chinese in Malaysia.

It is to be noted that the viability of the above-discussed value concepts in the maintenance of social order in the traditional Chinese life cannot be accurately assessed. Social cohesion was sought to be maintained by resorting to private mediation in a large number of cases. The chief characteristic was in seeking a compromise. This resulted in the reduced role of the courts in the administration of a justice system amongst the traditional Chinese in general.

NOTES

1   A traditional Chinese saying: *'heqing, heli, hefa'*.
2   Michael J. Moser, *Law And Social Change In A Chinese Community: A Case Study From Rural Taiwan*, Oceana Publications, New York, 1982, at page 60.
3   Clarence Bodde and Derk Morris, *Law In Imperial China*, Harvard University Press, Cambridge (Mass), 1967, at page 4. See also Geoffrey MacCormack, 'Natural Law and Cosmic Harmony in Traditional Chinese Thought' (1989) 2 *Ratio Juris*, 254; Geoffrey MacCormack, *The Spirit of Traditional Chinese Law*, The University of Georgia Press, Athens & London, 1996.
4   G. Jamieson, *Chinese Family And Commercial Law*, Vetch and Lee Limited, Hong Kong, 1970, at pages 1-2.
5   Clarence Bodde and Derk Morris, note 3 above, at page 4.
6   A good historical introduction regarding Chinese dispute resolution leading up to the Communist period is given in Stanley Lubman, 'Mao and Mediation: Politics and Dispute Resolution in Communist China' in (1967) 55 *California Law Review* at page 1289.
7   Stanley Lubman, note 6 above, at page 1294. See also Hu Chang-tu, *China - Its People, Its Society, Its Culture*, Hraf Press, New Haven, 1960, at pages 157-171; Kenneth Scott Latourette, *THE CHINESE, Their History and Culture*, Macmillan Company, New York, 1964, at pages 565-578.
8   Clarence Bodde and Derk Morris, note 3 above, at pages 5-6.
9   G. Jamieson, note 4 above, at pages 3-4.
10 Chu T'ung-tsu, *Law and Society in Traditional China*, Mouton & Co., Paris/La Haye, 1961, at page 279.
11 Hu Hsien-Chin (1948) at page 53 quoted in Sybille van der Sprenkel, *Legal Institutions in Manchu China: A Sociological Analysis*, University of London the Athlone Press, London, 1972, at page 31; Francis Fukuyama, *Trust: The Social Virtues and the Creation of Prosperity*, The Free Press, New York, 1995, at page 90.

12	Chu T'ung-tsu, note 10 above, at page 20; G. Jamieson, note 4 above, at page 2.
13	GOH Bee Chen, *Negotiating With The Chinese*, Dartmouth, Aldershot/Brookfield USA, 1996, at pages 51-52.
14	Sybille van der Sprenkel, note 11 above, at page 14.
15	Chu T'ung-tsu, note 10 above, at page 20.
16	In a family of many sons, the eldest son assumed this role.
17	Sybille van der Sprenkel, note 11 above, at pages 14-15. Chu T'ung-tsu appears to disagree on this point and insists that the father's authority must be exercised by a male (see Chu T'ung-tsu, note 10, at page 31). Hu Chang-tu is of the view that 'the head of the household was always a male unless no adult male survived': Hu Chang-tu, note 7 above, at page 159.
18	Hu Chang-tu, note 7 above, at pages 157-165.
19	G. Jamieson, note 4 above, at pages 2-3.
20	Chu T'ung-tsu, note 10 above, at page 29.
21	G. Jamieson, note 4 above, at pages 2-3.
22	Hu Chang-tu, note 7 above, at page 159; Sybille van der Sprenkel, note 11 above, at page 17.
23	James Legge (trans), *The Chinese Classics*, (1895) Vol. II, at page 313 quoted in H. McAleavy, 'Chinese Law In Hong Kong: The Choice of Sources' in J. N. D. Anderson (ed), *Hanging Law In Developing Countries*, George Allen & Unwin Ltd., London, 1963, at pages 262-263. See also Chu T'ung-tsu, note 10 above, at page 91.
24	*Hall v Wright* 120 ER 688, at page 695; *Hyde v Hyde* (1861-73) All ER 175, at page 177.
25	Chu T'ung-tsu, note 10 above, at page 91.
26	H. McAleavy, note 22 above, at pages 264-265. A good explanation is also given in Chu T'ung-tsu, note 10, at pages 124-125.
27	*Li Chi Chu-su*, quoted in Chu T'ung-tsu, note 10 above, at page 91.
28	Chu T'ung-tsu, note 10, at page 99. See also K. S. Latourette, note 7 above, at page 569.
29	Chu T'ung-tsu, note 10 above, at page 91.
30	H. McAleavy, note 22 above, at page 262.
31	H. McAleavy, note 22 above, at page 263; Hu Chang-tu, note 7, at page 160.
32	G. Jamieson, note 4 above, at page 3; Sybille van der Sprenkel, note 11 above, at pages 15-16. On the Chinese principles of adoption, see H. McAleavy, note 22 above, at page 263.
33	H. McAleavy, note 22 above, at pages 262-265; Sybille van der Sprenkel, note 11 above, at page 15.
34	Comment made by the late Tan Sri Lee Siow Mong, a local expert on Chinese Family and Customary Law in Malaysia. Interviewed on 8 July 1982 in Kuala Lumpur.
35	H. McAleavy, note 22 above, at page 264.

36   On this point of concubinage, in Malaysia, there seems to have been case-law misinterpretation of Chinese marriage law. As asserted by the late Tan Sri Lee Siow Mong, note 34 above, it is important to note that early Chinese Family Law allowed a man to have one wife and the other 'wives' were considered properly as concubines. Therefore, in actual fact, traditional Chinese custom did not allow polygamous marriages. But, the court in *The Six Widows Case* (1908) 12 SSLR 120 held that a Chinese man was polygamous. With the coming into force of the Law Reform (Marriage and Divorce) Act 1976 on 1 March 1982 in Malaysia, the non-Muslim Chinese matrimonial matters are governed by this statute. Section 5 of this Act purports to abolish polygamous marriages. This statutory intervention, in my view, is an example of the lack of legislative comprehension of Chinese personal customs.

37   Geoffrey MacCormack (1996), note 3 above, at page 10.

38   Chu T'ung-tsu, note 10 above, at page 103.

39   Chu T'ung-tsu, note 10 above, at page 103.

40   Chu T'ung-tsu, note 10 above, at page 103.

41   Geoffrey MacCormack (1996), note 3 above, at page 10.

42   Hu Chang-tu, note 7 above, at page 490.

43   For a comparison between the traditional Chinese family law and the ancient Roman law, *Patria Potestas*, see G. Jamieson, note 4 above, at pages 4-8.

44   G. Jamieson, note 4 above, at pages 159-160.

45   G. Jamieson, note 4 above, at pages 159-160.

46   G. Jamieson, note 4 above, at pages 159-160.

47   G. Jamieson, note 4 above, at pages 159-160. See also Sybille van der Sprenkel, note 11 above, at page 17.

48   K. S. Latourette, note 7 above, at page 566; Hu Chang-tu, note 7 above, at page 3.

49   K. S. Latourette, note 7 above, at page 568.

50   Sybille van der Sprenkel, note 11 above, at page 9.

51   Hu Chang-tu, note 7 above, at page 166.

52   Hu Chang-tu, note 7 above, at page 160; K. S. Latourette, note 7 above, at page 569; Chu T'ung-tsu, note 10 above, at pages 91-94.

53   There was a case in Paloh (a village in the State of Johore, Malaysia) in 1971 when my former classmate's brother could not marry a girl sharing the same surname (Chong). It was considered scandalous.

54   Hu Chang-tu, note 7 above, at page 6.

55   See Michael J. Moser, note 2 above, at page 118.

56   Sybille van der Sprenkel, note 11 above, at page 98; Michael J. Moser, note 2 above, at page 20.

57   John M. Koller, *Oriental Philosophies*, Charles Scribner's Sons, New

York, 1970, at page 214.

[58]   John M. Koller, note 57 above, at page 214.

[59]   John M. Koller, note 57 above, at page 215; H. McAleavy, note 22 above, at page 262. Van der Sprenkel argues that this English translated term is 'misleading' because *hsiao* also means 'complete submissiveness to one's seniors and superiors', see Sybille van der Sprenkel, note 11 above, at page 82, footnote 2.

[60]   James Legge, note 22 above, Vol. I, at page 147 quoted in H. McAleavy, note 22 above, at page 262.

[61]   See John M. Koller, note 57 above, at page 215: 'to protect the body is to honour the parents'.

[62]   John M. Koller, note 57 above, at pages 215-216.

[63]   *Analects* II:7, quoted in Wm Theodore de Barry, Chan Wing-tsit and Burton Watson (comp), *Sources of Chinese Tradition*, Columbia University Press, New York/London, 1966, at page 29.

[64]   Lee Yan Phou, *When I Was A Boy In China*, George G. Harrap & Co., London, 1935, at pages 21-22.

[65]   John M. Koller, note 57 above, at page 216.

[66]   John M. Koller, note 57 above, at pages 216-217.

[67]   John M. Koller, note 57 above, at page 216.

[68]   John M. Koller, note 57 above, at page 223.

[69]   Stanley Lubman, note 6 above, at page 1295.

[70]   See also Y. K. Leong and L. K. Tao, *Village And Town Life In China*, George Allen & Unwin Ltd., London, 1923, at page 16.

[71]   Sybille van der Sprenkel, note 11 above, at page 9.

[72]   Simon Roberts, *Order And Dispute: An Introduction To Legal Anthropology*, Penguin Books, Harmondsworth, 1979, at page 38.

[73]   Michael J. Moser, note 2 above, at page 20.

[74]   A.L. Epstein, *Contention And Dispute: Aspects of Law And Social Control In Melanesia*, Australian National University Press, Canberra, 1974, at page 23.

[75]   'Social Sanctions', *Encyclopaedia of the Social Sanctions*, Vol.13, at pages 531-534, quoted in Simon Roberts, note 72 above, at page 35.

[76]   Sybille van der Sprenkel, note 11 above, at page 98.

[77]   GOH Bee Chen, note 13 above, at page 95.

[78]   K. S. Latourette, note 7 above, at page 584.

[79]   Hu Chang-tu, note 7 above, at page 493.

[80]   Sybille van der Sprenkel, note 11 above, at page 99.

[81]   K. S. Latourette, note 7 above, at page 583.

[82]   Lucian Pye, *Chinese Negotiating Style: Commercial Approaches and Cultural Principles*, Quorum Books, New York et al., 1992, at page 101. See also Fanny M.C. Cheung, 'Psychopathy Among Chinese People' in Michael Harris Bond (ed), *The Psychology of the Chinese People*, Oxford University Press, Hong Kong, 1986, at pages 205-207.

83　Yunxiang Yan, *The Flow of Gifts: Reciprocity and Social Networks in a Chinese Village*, Stanford University Press, Stanford, 1996, at page 137.

84　Sybille van der Sprenkel, note 11 above, at page 99.

85　Hu Hsien-Chin gives a detailed exposition of *pu yao lien* in Sybille van der Sprenkel, note 11 above, at page 100.

86　Hu Hsien-Chin, quoted in Sybille van der Sprenkel, note 11 above, at page 100.

87　Yunxiang Yan, note 83 above, at page 137.

88　Yunxiang Yan, note 83 above, at page 137.

89　Paul S. Kirkbride and Sara F. Y. Tang, 'Negotiation: Lessons From Behind The Bamboo Curtain' (1990) 16 *Journal of General Management* 1, at page 7.

90　Yunxiang Yan, note 83 above, at page 138.

91　Michael Palmer provides an interesting case study in modern day China involving the principle of face-saving. See Michael Palmer, 'The Revival of Mediation in the People's Republic of China: (1) Extra-Judicial Mediation' in W.E. Butler (ed), *Yearbook on Socialist Legal Systems: 1987*, Transnational Publishers, Inc., Dobbs Ferry, New York, 1988, at pages 263-265.

92　Sybille van der Sprenkel, note 11 above, at page 25.

93　Sybille van der Sprenkel, note 11 above, at page 100; Stanley Lubman, note 6 above, at page 1294.

94　Stanley Lubman, note 6 above, at page 1294.

95　Sybille van der Sprenkel, note 11 above, at pages 100-101.

96　GOH Bee Chen, note 13 above, at page 98.

97　Lucian Pye, note 82 above, at page 101.

98　Michael J. Moser, note 3 above, at page 65.

99　GOH Bee Chen, note 13 above, at page 99.

100　GOH Bee Chen, note 13 above, at page 99.

101　Michael J. Moser, note 2 above, at page 65.

102　Yunxiang Yan, note 83 above, at page 146.

103　Michael J. Moser, note 2 above, at page 65.

104　Michael J. Moser, note 2 above, at page 68; GOH Bee Chen, note 13 above, at page 70.

105　See Michael Palmer, note 91 above, at page 233, where he observes that 'the traditional Confucian emphasis on yielding has been officially resurrected' in modern day China.

106　See Michael J. Moser, note 2 above.

107　See Yunxiang Yan, note 83 above.

108　See GOH Bee Chen, *The Traditional Chinese Concept of Law, Justice And Dispute Settlement, With Specific Reference To The Rural Chinese Malaysians*, Unpublished Project Paper, University of Malaya, 1982/83, Kuala Lumpur. See also Chapter 5, below.

109　See Kadir Kassim, 'Alternative Forum For The Settlement of

Disputes For The Common Man (In Malaysia)', paper presented at the ASEAN Law Association 1982 General Assembly on 26 October 1982 in Kuala Lumpur.

110   For instance, in Paloh in the State of Johore in Malaysia, the village where I was born, the majority of the Chinese parents are accustomed to sending their children to the Paloh Chinese Primary School.

4 Justice Without Courts

I desire... that those who have recourse to the tribunals should be treated without any pity, and in such a manner that they shall be disgusted with law, and tremble to appear before a magistrate.[1]

Introduction

The dominance of Confucian intellectual thought has been discussed in the previous Chapters. Suffice to say that the overriding stress on morality - rather than on law - was the principal tenet of Confucian teaching which resulted in the traditional preference for disputes and their settlement. As Lubman puts it, for the traditional Chinese, 'disputes were viewed as disruptions of the natural harmony which linked individual, group, society, and the entire universe'.[2] The best way to restore this harmony was through compromise.[3] There were in existence customary rules, social sanctions and ethical precepts which regulated the traditional Chinese society. At this juncture, one recalls the hierarchical structure of the Chinese society. The Chinese social hierarchy sought to instil in the individual a respect for authority. As seen earlier, in the traditional Chinese society, the family, rather than the individual, was considered as a unit. The family was deemed the foundation of the social order. Moreover, families were extended to include kinship organisations or clan groups. One of the duties of the clan (*tsu*) head was to maintain social harmony within his clan.[4] Such a unique feature evident in the traditional Chinese social structure coupled with Confucian ideology leaned favourably towards the informal process of dispute resolution. Furthermore, the members of the existing social units were educated in Confucian ideas of social conflict and morality. They were strongly encouraged to participate in social welfare work by helping the indigent and the infirm, establishing schools and maintaining places for ancestral worship, and settling disputes amongst the members.[5] As such, there was decidedly a preference for redress through the process of dispute resolution over litigation. Peaceable means of dispute settlement was definitely more desirable than any attempt at direct confrontation by way of court litigation.

In this Chapter, the traditional Chinese perception of how justice was to be administered will be raised. It is not intended to deal in detail with what justice means. It has been said that, for some, justice is an idea and an ideal.[6] Rather, what I propose to do here is to highlight the informal dispute settlement process as an effective means of obtaining justice in the preservation of social harmony and solidarity in the traditional Chinese society. The main point is that mediation or conciliation as the prime method of dispute resolution for the Chinese may be traced to the Chinese cultural tradition of preserving harmony, maintaining peace, and cultivating group solidarity through avoiding confrontation and engaging in aggression. Litigation, which epitomises the latter traits, has traditionally been viewed with suspicion and discomfort by the Chinese because it runs counter to the traditional Chinese social ideals as previously outlined.

Confucian Ideology And Dispute Settlement

In the Confucian view, the emergence of the formally-enacted law was an indication of moral decline. The Confucianist philosophy emphasizes a great deal on the cultivation of moral goodness. It is thought that a morally-disposed person presents a good role model for society as this culminates in the human embodiment of the principles of uprightness, justice and fairness, and considerations for the well-being for one's fellow humans. With regard to Law, the Confucianists maintained that 'the legal process was not one of the highest achievements of Chinese civilization but was, rather, a regrettable necessity'.[7] Phillip M. Chen also observes that 'Confucian values and heritage... put law in a very secondary, undesirable position'.[8] The tension between Morality and Law could not have been made more apparent by the conflicting schools of thought in Confucianism and Legalism.[9] As such, recourse to the courts was generally shunned. Instead, the traditional Chinese social structure consisting of various social groups - families, clans, villages, guilds - provided for the appropriate fora in favour of the mediational style of dispute settlement. In this regard, the application to the formal legal system was very rare.[10] Cohen further states that the fact that very few cases came before the courts 'provided a more accurate index of the Chinese predisposition to compromise'.[11] It can, therefore, be seen that the principle of compromise has been highly valued from the traditional times till today. The ability of the Chinese to compromise enables them to weigh mutual interests for the long term good, rather than rigidly adhering to the pursuit of individual rights at the expense of the communal or social interests. One is reminded of that fact that the Chinese are basically collectivists by nature. In this sense, it is important to always try to maintain group harmony. It is of less consequence that the individual's perceived rights may be subsumed because of the pre-occupation with social interests. Quite the contrary, it is a Confucian thing to do. Moser echoes a similar sentiment, as follows.

> Thus, the moral man's behaviour is directed toward promoting co-operation and solidarity by public example, rather than toward getting one's due.[12]

Such an attitude naturally contrasts sharply with the Western outlook. As we are well aware, in Western individualism, the pursuit of individual justice is the primary aim. Everything else is perceived as secondary. This is due to the fact that the self, rather than society, comes first. In dispute settlement, compromise requires one to meet the other mid-way, at the expense of one's just due. In this sense, the principle of compromise appears to be, *prima facie*, culturally incongruent to the individualist Westerner who is more used to the pursuit of individual justice. This may, in part, explain Boulle's concern that mediation in the West is 'a practice in search of a theory'.[13]

Confucianism advocated the principle that the preservation of harmony between humanity and nature, and as between humanity, was vital for the reason that 'the spheres of man and nature were thought of as forming a single continuum',[14] and, therefore, that social disharmony would lead to a violation of the total cosmic order.[15] The idea of litigation encouraged the pursuit of one's own interests at the expense of others.[16] As such, the process of dispute settlement which aimed at obtaining agreeable solutions and preserving harmonious relationships was consonant with the basic Confucian ideology.

'This attitude towards dispute settlement', Cohen writes, 'reflected the spirit of self-criticism the Confucian ideology sought to inculcate'.[17] This observation is largely true. One of the moral values that Confucius sought to teach was constant self-improvement of one's character through the process of self-criticism. A popular Chinese proverb provides for one to engage in constant meditation in order to reflect upon one's misdeeds and transgressions. It is thought that in this way, one can make reparations and redeem one's good character. Such an exercise reinforces the Confucian tenet of moral virtue. Therefore, in the traditional view, when the Confucian gentleman was unreasonably treated by another, he ought to regard it as a result of some personal failings on his part and to seek the source and solution of the problem. He would then be seen to be engaged in self-criticism, a first step towards the cultivation of moral virtue. Thus, by this process of self-improvement, a positive response might come about from the other party and the problem which could lead to a dispute would thereby be terminated even before it started. The emphasis here is dispute dissipation, which bears a preventative quality, rather than dispute resolution, which may be regarded as more remedial. In the Confucian view, a person was considered as morally disposed who did not insist on his rights but who preferred to settle a dispute through the means which enabled each other to save 'face'. To be conscious of and engaging in face-saving behaviour was certainly culturally desired. Translating a dispute into a lawsuit would cause one to lose 'face' because this implied a failing in one's virtue and moral standing, and an embarrassment that one did not command sufficient respect from the other as to elicit mutual concessions.[18] One was losing face for oneself and at the same time causing the other person to lose face. Viewed in this light, moral persuasion was highly valued.

Disputes, which ultimately meant a disturbance of the social as well as the natural order, were to be avoided if possible. Reconciliation took precedence over direct confrontation. The virtue of *rang* (or yielding), a common social sanction, was strongly encouraged to ward off 'friction and disharmony'.[19] Van der Sprenkel states, in connection with *rang*, that it was better 'to meet an opponent half-way than to stand on principle'.[20] The virtue of *rang* essentially accounted for the Chinese preference for compromise. Effectively, what was socially desired was the observance of compromise thus leading to the preservation of harmony. This was in accordance with the Confucian *li*, an embodiment of proper rules of behaviour, ethical principles and ceremonial rites. Besides, as Cohen rightly points out, 'Confucian values emphasized not the rights of the individual but the functioning of the social order',[21] and even if one was clearly in the right, it was better, for the sake of group solidarity, to forgive the offender than to 'exact one's pound of flesh'.[22] To reiterate, the social value for the traditional Chinese is founded upon communal interests, not individual needs. Mediation or conciliation serves this group principle, and is, therefore, preferred.

Based on the foregoing, it thus appears that the Confucian philosophic thought and the dispute resolution method concur in the ideas of harmony and compromise. What next needs to be examined is the organizational context of the traditional institutions in old China from which this mode of dispute settlement found its favourable beginning.

Traditional Chinese Social Institutions In Aid of Dispute Settlement

'In traditional China,' Lubman writes, 'a great gulf divided state and society'.[23] This requires some explanation. Properly speaking, the traditional Chinese had no concept of society because such a concept arose as a Western phenomenon. It has been seen earlier in Chapter 3 that the importance of the family in the traditional Chinese way of life was unparalleled in any other civilization. One again needs to remind oneself that the family, in the Chinese sense, actually comprised larger kin groups. There was, in reality, therefore, no need for the concept of 'society' as such. Moreover, village ties in traditional China were very strong.[24] People who came from the same village were considered as from one clan, or *tsu*. This again ruled out the need for the Western sense of society because the concept of the Chinese family constituted one large 'society'. This point may be made clearer by referring to the Chinese phrase, *kuo-chia*, literally taken to mean 'country-family', 'nation-family' or 'state-family'. The phrase shows that the Chinese individual did not consider himself as a unit, but rather, he associated himself at once with the family. From the family, the next immediate unit was the country/nation/state to which his allegiance was owed. It was within this premise that the Confucian emphasis on the proper regulation of the family leading to the well-being of the state established its root.[25]

In traditional China, the existing social institutions - the family, the clan, the village, the guild, the gentry and so on - played an important role in dispute resolution. Such social institutions held 'informal sway' in the ordinary person's life and 'helped to smooth the inevitable frictions in Chinese society by inculcating moral precepts upon their members, mediating disputes, or, if need arose, imposing disciplinary sanctions and penalties'.[26] Their role frequently outweighed the role of the formal courts of law. Moreover, litigants dreaded the courts because of the humiliation experienced and the fact that they were at the mercies of the Magistrate and his underlings. At this juncture, one is not surprised to draw the conclusion that such forensic humiliation was deliberate. Support for this proposition can be found in the decree of Emperor Kang-hsi (reigned 1662-1723) of the Qing Dynasty (1644-1911):

> ...lawsuits would tend to increase to a frightful amount, if people were not afraid of the tribunals, and if they felt confident of always finding in them ready and perfect justice. As man is apt to delude himself concerning his own interests, contests would then be interminable, and half of the Empire would not suffice to settle the lawsuits of the other half. I desire, therefore, that those who have recourse to the tribunals should be treated without pity, and in such a manner that they shall be disgusted with law, and tremble to appear before a Magistrate.[27]

The official authority, therefore, did not favour litigation as a means of terminating disputes. The Emperor commended the good subjects on their ability to settle disputes amicably 'like brothers' and chided that 'for those who are troublesome, obstinate and quarrelsome, let them be ruined in the law-courts - that is the justice that is due to them'.[28] Given that the traditional attitude towards the law courts has been so devastatingly negative, it is little wonder that the same has been passed down the generations of Chinese to the modern day. The fear of the law courts has been portrayed as a real fear to be considered by the average Chinese to be imbibed with danger ('weixian').

The following is a study of the traditional Chinese social institutions and their role in the dispute settlement process.

The Gentry

Hu Chang-tu calls the gentry 'the scholar-official class'.[29] This interpretation is not always accurate. As Lubman more rightly observes, the gentry were the scholars who had to pass the Imperial Examinations on the Confucian classics but might not hold office in every case.[30] From another point of view, van der Sprenkel offers a variety of qualities which made up the gentry as a class. Some of these qualities were:

(a)   wealth, viz. ownership of property and size of income;
(b)   marital success, by avoiding connection with any shameful act such as divorce, or frequently indulging in quarrels;
(c)   conformity with socially approved code of conduct, by being filial and obedient within one's family, and generous with gifts during festivities, marriages or births in a local society;
(d)   the leisure that one could frequently spare in participating in tea-shop discussions;
(e)   education, since 'so many were completely illiterate'.[31]

Education has always been regarded as the prime prestige factor in the Chinese way of life, both traditional and modern. As Hu Chang-tu points out, 'in China it was not land or birth as in Europe but education which created the gentry as a class' and he goes on to observe, 'success in the examinations could bring a man, even of humble origin, legally privileged status, social prestige, access to a career in officialdom, and the means of acquiring wealth'.[32] In short, the gentry constituted the elite of the traditional Chinese society, acquiring the same status as the officials. As a result, the gentry and their families were highly respected, and were very influential. Besides, the gentry played the intermediary role: the common folk often channelled their grievances to the officials through the gentry, and the officials used the gentry to detect the grouses of the peasantry.[33]

On the settlement of disputes, the gentry were often seen to be pre-occupied with this function.[34] Some of them even became over-zealous, and were criticized as standing to gain from settling disputes, or stirring up the disputes themselves.[35]

From the cultural viewpoint, the position of the gentry serves to highlight the hierarchical nature of the traditional Chinese society. Their rank or status in the community enabled them to carry out the quasi-adjudicatory functions.

The Village Leaders

In this category were included the village headmen and other informal leaders. They, too, were influential people who commanded respect or awe of the village folk in general. On this basis, they exercised considerable power over the common people, and their authority in the process of dispute resolution was frequently obeyed. Here, too, we witnessed another layer of the traditional Chinese social hierarchy.

The village acted as a unit in most cases. The traditional village consisting of only the family with one surname was regarded as 'a common descent group',[36] i.e. from the same *tsu* (or clan). In other cases, village unity was very common, too. For example, the dispute of an individual of one village with a member of another village could easily develop into an inter-village dispute: 'If a dispute arose between Chang of village A and Wang of village B as to where the exact boundary of their holdings (i.e. village frontiers) lay, this would involve not only the two individuals concerned, and their families, but might easily develop into a dispute between their two villages'.[37] Such an occurrence should not come across as surprising, given the communal nature of the Chinese and their essential homocentricity.

Because the village might also mean the *tsu*, 'village leadership and lineage structure' appeared to be connected.[38] The authority of the village headman facilitated the settlement of disputes between the disputants. Frequently, the principle of *ganqing*[39] was involved. For example, if a village headman was invited to 'hear' a dispute, he would try to resolve it amicably by asking the disputants to consider *ganqing* between themselves, or requesting them to terminate the dispute on the basis of his *ganqing* with both of them.[40] This was made possible due to the close relationship between the parties. The family ties had to be preserved. More importantly, harmony must be restored. What was secondary was the consideration of any perceived individual justice.

Apart from the village headman of a given village, there were other informal leaders who assisted in settling disputes. They were 'respected because of their age, learning, and reputation for probity, or feared because of their aggressiveness and unscrupulousness'.[41]

The Families And Clans

The family (clan included) was the basic unit of the traditional Chinese society, the importance of which has been dealt with in the foregoing Chapter. Here, it is attempted to examine the role of the families and clans in the settlement of disputes.

Within the small family itself, the authority of the *chia chang* was obeyed, and he held control and general superintendence of family matters. Van der Sprenkel writes, 'the inculcation of personal virtues - such as filial piety, deferring to one's seniors, supporting parents in old age, the merits of *rang* - that is, yielding to others for the sake of avoiding dissension - began in childhood in the constituent *chia*, lapses being punished by the *chia chang*, by a sort of delegated political authority'.[42] This shows the family as a social control unit in the traditional Chinese way of life. Needless to say, the family assumed fundamental importance in settling disputes amongst the members within it.[43]

As for the *tsu*, one of the primary duties of the *tsu* head was to preserve social harmony within the *tsu* itself. He was also responsible for settling inter-family quarrels. In most cases, he acted as 'judge and arbitrator' and was regarded as 'the supreme judicial authority' within his clan.[44]

A Chinese saying to the effect that 'family ignominy should not be published to the outsider'[45] illustrates the Chinese concern for 'face' and the effectiveness of dispute resolution as a means of control mechanism within the family or clan. This view is further supported by the fact that the so-called rules of the clan very often forbade its members to get involved in litigation; rather, they had first to submit their case to the clan leaders. They were strongly discouraged by the *tsu* rules from getting entangled in disputes within or without the *tsu*.[46]

The Guilds

These formed part of the traditional Chinese social institutions through which extra-legal redress could be sought.[47] A guild was an association of tradesmen or artisans belonging to the same trade or craft. At times, it could be formed as a 'quasi-insurance' measure against unbearable financial responsibility, or labour shortage in seasonal work.[48] Most matters of the various callings were governed by the respective guilds. These included price regulation, apprenticeship, competition and admission. These guilds were quite well-known in their charitable ventures and philanthropic objects.[49]

Van der Sprenkel points out that Western observers have been surprised by Chinese 'reticence' on commercial laws when the latter were reputable for their business acumen. Such a reticence would not have surprised the interested Westerner if he or she had examined the internal regulations of the guilds concerned.[50] Such regulations were often detailed, stringent, and they provided for internal dispute settlement. There was no need to invoke the help of the formal courts, unless exceptional circumstances existed which went beyond the power of the guilds to control.

Another type of association arose in old China. It had been well-established that persons who came from the same area in China and who subsequently found themselves in a new place strange to its 'people, custom and perhaps even dialect' readily grouped together 'for mutual support and companionship'.[51] This sort of clannishness lent to the group a kind of solidarity in times of need and also helped troubled members in settling disputes for them.

The above general survey of the traditional Chinese social institutions makes it hardly surprising that the traditional Chinese have, since early times, allowed their ideology (i.e. Confucian views on social harmony and compromise) to interact with the existing institutions to give rise to their strong preference for private mediation. Moreover, these institutions were, to the laymen, extra-legal organs with comprehensible procedures, and, as such, they were normally availed upon by the common folk for 'guidance and sanction, rather than to the formal judicial system per se'.[52] What needs present attention, therefore, is an analysis of the process of dispute settlement.

Dispute and Settlement

It is proposed to discuss this topic by dealing with three specific areas:

> Mediation v. Litigation
> Traditional modes of dispute settlement
> Imperfections and Benefits of dispute settlement

The rationale in dividing this discussion into three specific areas is to attempt to obtain maximum insight into the traditional Chinese dispute resolution method and arrive at a critical assessment of it.

Mediation v. Litigation

In any society, mediation and litigation are viewed as two various means of obtaining redress. In traditional China, there existed a strong preference for mediation, i.e. to obtain redress through peaceful means and by amicable settlement. Various reasons can be put forth as to why mediation took precedence over litigation in the traditional Chinese society, and they are examined as follows.

To begin with, the traditional Chinese society was predominantly influenced by Confucian thought which valued moral principles and had little regard for legal measures. As a result, the formal law was hardly invoked. Concurrently, the official government discouraged litigation, encouraged the disputants to yield ground and compromise wherever possible, and emphasised greatly on the ideal of non-contentiousness.

In this regard, one needs to bear in mind the fact that the social ideal for harmony took precedence over the individual desires. The Confucian tenet of *ho*, meaning harmony, which we saw in Chapter 2, has sought to provide an entrenched value in the traditional Chinese society. Mediation, as a means of dispute settlement, therefore, came to be seen as hand-in-glove with this ideal of social harmony. This was made possible by the requirements for, and, expectations of compromise. Over the centuries, what in the West was held as sacrosanct in terms of the preservation of individual justice did not attain the same status in traditional China. An insistence on individual justice would be, *prima facie*, contrary to the need to compromise for the sake of preserving social harmony, to which the traditional Chinese had grown accustomed.

Mediation was also preferred because litigation possessed many inherent defects. There did not exist in old China the status profession in the Law as found in the Occidental legal profession. In the West, the legal profession has always been considered a noble and well-respected one. The legal profession, in traditional Chinese thinking, was fraught with immorality. One must recall that the emergence of law in ancient China meant a moral decline as well. Thus, the legal profession was not spared the connotation of immorality. Another taint of immorality was the Chinese belief that human mischief would be punished accordingly by the will of Heaven, but the fact that lawyers could wrangle with the tenets of the law to achieve personal ends was viewed with horror. ˡ ˡisconsultˢ ˡ[53] and the underlings of the magistracy often taught the litigants the means to fabricate evidence, twist facts, and tell lies in the court in order to win their lawsuit. Moreover, although a person might not be directly involved in a case he could be subpoenaed to testify against a relative or friend: such betrayal, too, was considered immoral in Chinese eyes.[54]

The so-called administrators of justice were not, properly speaking, legally-trained personnel.[55] It was not uncommon for the magistrates themselves to plead ignorance of the law upon which the case of the litigants depended. The former were frequently preoccupied with other sorts of administrative functions and, therefore, suffered the cases to be dealt with by their subordinates.[56] Corruption was rampant and it has been said that 'the verdict often went to the longest purse'.[57] A Chinese proverb testifies to the unpopularity of the *yamen*, or the court: 'If the six doors of the *yamen* are open wide, those who have right on their side but have no money will not enter'.[58] Moreover, the *yamen* was often situated afar, and this inevitably involved travelling expenses.[59] Delays were not uncommon and any error in the judicial process often meant that the litigant would then fall prey to the whims and fancies of the court officials.[60]

Court trials were invariably humiliating, not only for the litigants, but the witnesses, too. The traditional Chinese system did not possess the English system of adversarial justice but rather, the court proceedings were structured 'to emphasize the unworthiness of all... persons'[61] and, as such, torture was used to elicit evidence or a confession of guilt.[62] The litigants and the witnesses had to kneel before the presiding magistrate, while the other court officials looked on 'menacingly'.[63] This, in the ultimate analysis, instilled fear in the parties concerned in order to arouse regard for the supremacy of the law.[64] In connection with the Chinese prison, Bird describes thus: 'If crime, vice, despair, suffering, filth, and cruelty can make a hell on earth, this is one'.[65] This goes to show the wretched prison conditions in old China. Moreover, the prisoners whom she saw comprised the criminals and 'hostages' for criminal relations who were still at large. It appeared that such hostages were legally prescribed. All of them had to undergo misery and torture.[66] It is little wonder that the official legal machinery came across as the last resort, and why the Chinese have traditionally harboured an intense dislike and suspicion for the courts and the formal adjudicatory process.

As the Chinese legal codes were penal in emphasis and no distinction was made between the criminal and the civil, the natural result that followed was that the form of all judicial proceedings was 'accusatory'.[67] The institution of a legal suit would, in all cases, entail punishment for either the 'plaintiff' or the 'defendant'. As is well-observed by van der Sprenkel, '[a legal case] could end in punishment for the accused, if judged guilty; if he were not, punishment would be assigned to the unjustified accuser'.[68] Such a system might appear to be absurd to the observer trained in a Western system of law, but the justification for it was to be found in the principle of preserving natural harmony. This, as explained by van der Sprenkel, was attributed to the strong Chinese belief in the existence of natural harmony in the human world and a lack of perception of individual human rights, with the end result that someone must shoulder the responsibility of having disturbed the natural order because the institution of a legal suit was 'seen as an indication of disturbance, and some action had to be taken to restore the situation'.[69]

Generally speaking, the Chinese had little confidence in the formal judicial process. Various Chinese proverbial sayings have grown out of such a lack of faith, and these proverbs help in reminding the Chinese people that litigation is to be avoided at all costs.[70] Some instances of such proverbs are:

(a)   'To enter a court of law is to enter a tiger's mouth';
(b)   'Inform against a man once and three generations of his family will become your enemies';
(c)   'Of ten reasons by which a magistrate may decide a case, nine are unknown to the public';
(d)   'Let householders avoid litigation; for once go to law and there is nothing but trouble'.[71]

In short, litigation was tainted with the notion of immorality, time-consuming, filled with corrupt practices, costly, humiliating, and opposed to the Chinese world view. What Phillip M. Chen states was largely true:

One of the reasons that Chinese people do not like adjudication is that control of the dispute leaves their hands.

Moreover, the Chinese traditionally have felt that going to court for a decision means that, even if you are the aggrieved party, you do lose face - going to court is an admission that the other person does not have sufficient respect for you to settle properly outside the court.[72]

Furthermore, litigation was, to a great extent, widely discouraged by the 'basic nuclei'[73] of the ancient Chinese society. The social units within the nuclei ensured that all forms of other available remedies were exhausted before the magistrate's justice was sought. As Lubman points out, 'if disputes could not be settled within the unit, relatives, friends, and local leaders outside the group, but still closer to the disputants than the magistrate, would often resolve them by mediation'.[74] In this connection, it is pertinent, too, to take note of the general Chinese fear of an involvement with the bureaucracy and the government officials[75] - the court, being a part of the bureaucratic machinery, represented, to the Chinese, one of the three great taboos, the other two being the undertaker (symbolic of death) and the pawnshop (indicative of debt).[76]

Traditional Modes of Dispute Settlement

Why has mediation been favoured? As a general rule, mediation encourages open discussion and much talk is exchanged. This process of meeting and talking helps to bring about an agreeable compromise and acceptable solution to the disputants. Simon Roberts explains the advantage of talking in human interaction thus: 'through talk people get to know what others are thinking and are going to do, as well as how their own actions are perceived, and are enabled to arrange their affairs accordingly'.[77] This observation is generally true as regards the traditional Chinese who relied heavily on talking in the mediation process to help the disputants settle their case amicably.[78]

Van der Sprenkel puts forth the principal methods of traditional dispute settlement and categorizes them into four - negotiation, mediation/conciliation, arbitration, enquiry - of which the first three were more relevant, as the fourth would suggest the intervention of a government body. To discuss in some detail, the first three processes were stated as:

(a)   negotiation - no outside help was sought. The disputants arrived at a settlement between themselves;

(b)   mediation or conciliation - the help of a third party would be sought who would attempt to help the disputants reach a compromise without dictating terms to them;

(c)   arbitration - there was a kind of a 'hearing' by the third party, who then pronounced his judgment and made an award, which would be abided by due to the arbitrator's inherent authority.[79]

These methods, in certain cases, could hardly be distinguished, and, their distinction became more fine than real. As van der Sprenkel herself has pointed out, 'the form of intervention ranged from completely private mediation at one end of the scale to public adjudication at the other, the one shading into the other almost imperceptibly as public opinion was felt to be more strongly involved'.[80] In other words, the disputants might begin negotiating between themselves, but the final outcome of their dispute might be determined by an external agency.

A disputant might call on a third party to conciliate the dispute on the basis of the latter's friendship or personal connection (i.e. *guanxi*) with him, or with the other disputing party, or because the third party was in some way involved in the dispute, for instance, as a witness to the transaction. Quite possibly, a third party might wish to act as a mediator out of his own volition, in the expectation to gain, or because he felt duty-bound to get a relative or friend out of the dispute.[81]

A family dispute would, most probably, be settled within the family by the family elder. A dispute arising from the clan would be resolved by the clan leaders, or other local leaders. Village disputes would be mediated by kinsmen, friends, neighbours, the gentry, some other respected village personalities and even by the government-appointed headmen who came to be personally respected by the villagers. Within the guilds, the guild officer would handle the dispute only after any attempts at mediation by friends or witnesses were unsuccessful.[82]

With specific reference to the clan, some, if not most, clan rules totally prohibit litigation. The rule stipulated would read thus: 'Throughout the *tsu* it is forbidden to stir up litigation. When people are angry with each other for a time, it rests with the mediators to arbitrate and bring about a conciliation'.[83] The clan rule further recognized the fact that such a prohibition was necessary because there were people who liked to stir up trouble for personal ends, who enjoyed seeing others suffer, and, therefore, such unscrupulousness had to be brought under control. In old China, as one ought to be aware, to be summoned before the *tsu* head in itself was a humiliation. The most severe sanction inflicted took the form of expulsion from the *tsu*. This meant complete isolation. 'For a Chinese this would represent failure in the most important things in life, and without the support of his own relatives, it would be difficult to make a success of anything else'.[84] Sincere repentance by the guilty offender followed by a reparation of his conduct might be strong inducement for his re-admission into his *tsu*. It is to be noted that the staunchness of the *tsu* as an institution differed in the various parts of old China, but *tsu* influence was particularly strong in South China, especially in the Provinces of Fukien and Guangtung[85] - the reason being that most of the villages in these two provinces were clan communities.[86]

The process of mediation has been described as follows. The village leaders, whether invited or self-appointed, would first attempt to find out the background leading to the dispute, and would then focus on what was really in issue. The opinions of other villagers would also be taken into account as to how the dispute actually arose. Then, a solution would be proposed based on the past experience of the village leaders. It was at this stage that the 'mediators had to shuttle between the [disputing] parties'[87] in order to help them arrive at a compromise. Having arrived at an agreeable solution, a feast would ensue. The mediators, the village leaders, the clan heads, and the heads of the two disputing families, (sometimes the close friends of the disputants), partook of the feast which symbolically concluded the dispute. Everything else but the dispute might be discussed at the feast. If, clearly, there was only one party at fault, he would have to bear the total expenses of the feast. If both parties had been found to be equally unreasonable, and both admitted their wrongs, the expense would be shared between them. And, if the mediators did not propose a solution because one party voluntarily conceded, or involuntarily surrendered to the opponent, the yielding party would have to bear the entire cost of the feast. The conflict was thus publicly concluded.[88]   Compensation was rarely asked because it was considered 'undignified',[89] even among the poor peasantry. It was, however, quite common to offer the mediating tea as 'compensation', but not in the pecuniary sense.[90] The compensation here referred to the non-pecuniary restoration of face.[91] It has been observed that in a Chinese village, a teahouse was specially set up for use by the village leaders in mediating disputes.[92] One other common means of 'compensation' was the offer of a public apology.[93] Pecuniary compensation would be relevant if money issues were involved, such as debts, or medical expenses if physical injury had been inflicted which required medical treatment.

The termination of the dispute with a feast, as illustrated above, marked the victory of the party in the right, in the sense that public opinion was on his side, and this 'public opinion' was often more cherished than any monetary compensation, because he had to upkeep his 'face' and secure his respect among his fellow members, preferably, at all times.[94]

The idea of the feast was both practical and symbolic in that it signified the 'public' nature of a dispute and a demonstration that social harmony was the desired goal. Feasting was also seen as a pleasurable activity, thereby acting as a sweetening end to the sour relations experienced during disputing. The feast also served to restore the 'face' of the disputants, a public indication that the past was forgiven, and the future should augur well again.

In this connection, van der Sprenkel has keenly observed that the idea of the feast served to penalize the offender, to remind him and the community at large of the rule that he had breached, and, above all, to re-integrate the members and strengthen community solidarity 'by joint participation in an enjoyable activity',[95] and she goes on to add, 'by making the wrong-doer provide a feast or entertainment for the group, they gave him the chance to compensate for his recent loss of reputation. Not only was he accepted back into the group after estrangement, but he was restored to general favour by playing the honourable role of host to the whole membership'.[96] In this way, social harmony was preserved and group solidarity strengthened.

In the words of another commentator, Hsiao:

> The feast that came at the end of the negotiation not only served to formalize the settlement, but at the same time to provide a friendly atmosphere (or a semblance of it), as a token that the bad feelings formerly existing between the disputants were now patched up. The wine cup, in a way, was the Chinese version of the 'peace pipe' of North America.[97]

Another writer, Fried,[98] who has conducted his study in Anhwei (in east central China) suggests three ways of handling 'civil' disputes thus: first, the parties would try to settle their dispute on the basis of *ganqing,* and this meant an appeal to the affection. Failing this method, then, the mediators would appeal to reason. A considered judgment would then be proposed to the disputants. The last method i.e. by taking the matter to the court, was 'anathema'[99] to the common folk.

Within the clans and the guilds, Lubman points out that some of the procedures adopted were similar to 'arbitration and adjudication',[100] in cases where private mediation had become unsuccessful. This meant that a formal hearing would be conducted in the clan hall in the presence of a team of clan leaders, or, as in the case of the guild, in the guild hall before a group of guild officers.[101] The difference in such a procedure being that evidence would be elicited through the disputing parties and witnesses giving their testimony, and the clan head or guild leader would then impose a decision.

In all other cases of mediation, no decision was imposed, rather, a compromise solution would be proposed subject to the acceptance of the disputants. Granted that the imposition of a decision might be necessary in more difficult cases, the prevailing ideas of dispute settlement would prefer these mediators to help the parties arrive at a compromise without forcing a decision on them.[102]

However, in the case of the traditional mediation practised by the Chinese, one could hardly discern the voluntariness in the acceptance of the solution reached at the conclusion of a mediation. More often than not, the solution was 'imposed'. A mediator who was highly regarded socially could not be seen to have his reasoned suggestions or proposals at a settlement defied by the disputants. This would cause a considerable loss of face to the mediator. Public opinion would then mean that it was the mediator's face at stake, and the private dispute would be reduced in significance. It was not surprising then for a settlement proposal to be accepted just so that the *guanxi* was not jeopardised, the *ganqing* was maintained and the *renqing* held intact. These were the unconscious social sanctions operating at a powerful and subtle level in order to achieve an amicable end. All this makes sense when viewed in light of the great importance of social harmony which was cherished by the community far more than anything else.

Imperfections and Benefits of Dispute Settlement

No system can be absolutely perfect. Although it is conceded that the traditional Chinese means of extra-legal access to justice appeared to yield many advantages (to be discussed later), it, too, suffered from certain ills. As Hsiao says, traditional mediation 'was not an all-sufficient social instrument'.[103]

'Just as the magistrate was often not a model Confucian gentleman', Lubman points out, 'so the extra-judicial mediator was not always an exemplar of Confucian virtue'.[104] As to be noted, some mediators might themselves stir up trouble for personal gains.[105] The 'profits' might be pecuniary profits or an increase of 'face' because 'the fact of being asked to conduct negotiations in itself conferred a certain amount of 'face', as it showed confidence in [the mediators'] ability and trustworthiness'.[106] This want of scruple on the part of the mediators greatly undermined the ideal dispute resolution method.

Unfairness was not peculiar to the formal courts alone.[107] The peace-talking could sometimes be unevenly balanced, showing the mediator's favouritism to either of the disputing parties, especially when one party was more powerful (in terms of wealth or status) than the other. Corruption and certain other perverted practices could be spotted. Unfairness could occur through the parties' anxiety to terminate the dispute, and accept whatever that was proposed. This anxiety came about as a result of a negative regard for disputes, that disputes were embarrassing, degrading and distressing. The risk involved in wanting to dispose of the dispute too quickly was that the conflict might not have been properly resolved, resulting in the persistence of the disagreement which would explode in a bigger form at a future date.[108]

Although mediation might succeed in terminating disputes, it did not always mean that inter-personal harmony was restored. As Hsiao incisively remarks:

> Disputes were after all symptomatic of maladjusted personal relationships between the inhabitants of a community or of deep-seated social discord that inhered in the neighbourhoods or in the larger society. After conflicts had come to the surface and became serious enough to call for intercession, it might be quite impossible really to heal the breach. In the general social context of imperial China, compromise was more valuable as a technique of stopping

rifts from developing into violent struggles, of minimizing the detrimental effects of conflicts, than as a positive method of preserving social harmony.[109]

Furthermore, the final outcome of the dispute, when a settlement was reached, invariably ended in a feast. This entailed considerable costs and expenses. For the relatively poor, such an expense could be ill-afforded. Therefore, the risk of expense was common in both the dispute settlement process and in the formal law courts.[110]

In ancient China, the process of dispute settlement often precluded the party's right of appeal to the official court when dissatisfied with the community judgment. If he chose to go against such judgment, he would be considered as flouting public opinion,[111] and not merely challenging his opponent alone. Moreover, the magistrate would readily concur with the community leaders and this, in turn, meant that the guilt of the appealing party was pre-determined before his case was heard. The appeal would, in any way, be futile.[112]

Imperfections aside, the usefulness of the mediation process was its most attractive attribute. Indeed, it was regarded as 'an integral feature of Chinese society'.[113] Some salient advantages were:

Firstly, the disputants were put at ease to bargain with one another in order to come to a compromise acceptable to both;

Secondly, there was no, or if any, little, fear and menacing attitude to disrupt the rationality of the disputants;

Thirdly, heavy litigation expenses were avoided;

Fourthly, the principle of social harmony was preserved. This was considered by far the most desirable social goal;

Fifthly, it provided 'a method of terminating disputes that was socially acceptable in the light of the Confucian ethic and group mores'[114] and also provided ancillary support for the dissemination and inculcation of Confucian virtues. One recalls that mediators played an instructive and educative role;

Lastly, the burden of the law-courts was considerably reduced, and friction between the common people and the magistracy kept to a minimum.[115]

Conclusion

Justice without courts, in traditional China, was a prevalent practice. The idea of a continuum between humanity and nature categorically expressed the significance of the traditional dispute settlement process. Between the disputing parties, there should be no standard for what was right or wrong, and since everybody was positioned within this continuum, what really mattered was the approval of the disputants standing in a definite relationship to each other, and to the community at large. The notion of *rang* (yielding) was a positive sign: a party forsaking something, might, in another way, acquire something else. To yield to another, when the circumstances so required, denoted the greatness of the person, and showed him or her to be of modest, humble and respectful conduct. A Confucian, indeed.

What was paramount was the concept of harmony, in its widest possible sense. In this regard, litigation which stood at the opposite end of the concept of harmony was abhorred.

The ordinary affairs of the lay persons had little to do with the official legal system. Other supportive social factors such as the prevailing customs, the moral and ethical precepts and the non-administrative agencies found in the social units discussed above played a far more vital role in the everyday life of the common folk. The matters which principally preoccupied the legal and judicial professionals in the West were, in traditional China, the concern of the social units. Although the Chinese customs might vary in the different parts of China, they were sufficiently well-known in their respective localities. This facilitated their enforcement.

Public opinion constituted a strong sanction and, in this way, the authority of the local leaders was obeyed. Any 'punishment' inflicted was aimed at preserving the harmony of the considered whole. The idea of providing a feast was an ingenious device in the attempt to restore social harmony, encourage group solidarity and promote communal cohesion. It was also very common to offer 'mediating tea' which represented the lowest form of 'damages'.[116]

In assessing the role of the Chinese courts, one has to bear in mind that they have never attained the same status as the Western courts. As has been aptly said by van der Sprenkel, for the Chinese 'the courts were not a vehicle for the expression of aspirations, nor an engine of social change'.[117] This naturally leads one to the conclusion that a study of the Chinese legal tradition and the Common Law Justice system will, in all probability, bring out more contrasts than comparisons.

Earlier, it was raised that the importance of the clan was particularly emphasised in South China. Considering the fact that the majority of the Chinese Malaysians are descendants of the South China dialectal groups, the above observations on the traditional Chinese concepts of Law and Justice, and the dispute settlement process pertaining to the rural Chinese Malaysians will be the subject of study in the next Chapter. It will be interesting to examine whether, and to what extent, tradition persists to the present.

NOTES

[1]   Emperor Kang-his (reigned 1662-1723). Quoted in Sybille van der Sprenkel, *Legal Institutions In Manchu China: A Sociological Analysis*, University of London, The Athlone Press, London, 1962, at page 77.

[2]   See Stanley Lubman, 'Mao and Mediation: Politics and Dispute Resolution In Communist China' (1967) 55 *California Law Review* at page 1291. This article gives a good historical introduction regarding Chinese dispute resolution leading up to the Communist period.

[3]   See Jerome Alan Cohen, 'Chinese mediation on the Eve of Modernization' (1966) 54 *California Law Review* at page 1207 where the author gives an excellent account of 'traditional Chinese mediation'.

[4]   Chu T'ung-tsu, *Law And Society In Traditional China*, Mouton & Co., Paris/La Haye, 1961, at page 37.

[5]   Stanley Lubman, note 2 above, at page 1294. See also Y. K. Leong and L. K. Tao, *Village And Town Life In China*, George Allen & Unwin Ltd., London, 1923, at pages 24-25.

[6]   For a detailed discussion on this point, see Eugene Kamenka, 'What is Justice?' in Eugene Kamenka and Alice Erh-Soon Tay (eds), *Ideas And Ideologies: JUSTICE*, Edward Arnold, London, 1977, at pages 1-24.

[7]   Jerome A. Cohen, note 3 above, at page 1206.

8   Phillip M. Chen, *Law and Justice: The Legal System In China 2400 B.C. To 1960 A.D.*, Dunellen Publishing Company, New York, 1973, at page 7.

9   Michael J. Moser, *Law And Social Change In a Chinese Community: A Case Study From Rural Taiwan*, Oceana Publications, Inc., New York, 1982, at page 61.

10   Phillip M. Chen, note 8 above, at page 7; Sybille van der Sprenkel, note 1 above, at page 101.

11   Jerome A. Cohen, note 3 above, at page 1210.

12   Michael J. Moser, note 9 above, at page 62.

13   Laurence Boulle, *Mediation: Principles, Process, Practice*, Butterworths, Sydney, 1996, at page v.

14   Derk Bodde and Clarence Morris, *Law In Imperial China*, Harvard University Press, Cambridge (Massachusetts), 1967, at page 43.

15   Derk Bodde and Clarence Morris, note 14 above, at pages 43-44; Jerome A. Cohen, note 3 above, at page 1207; Sybille van der Sprenkel, note 1 above, at page 29; Stanley Lubman, note 2 above, at page 1290; Phillip M. Chen, note 8 above, at pages 14-15.

16   Jerome A. Cohen, note 3 above, at page 1207. In this connection, see also Stanley B. Lubman and Gregory c. Wajnowski, 'International Commercial Dispute Resolution In China' (1993) *American Review of International Arbitration* 107, at page 111.

17   Jerome A. Cohen, note 3 above, at page 1207.

18   Jerome A. Cohen, note 3 above, at pages 1207-1208; see also Phillip M. Chen, note 8 above, at pages 3-4.

19   Stanley Lubman, note 2 above, at page 1291.

20   Sybille van der Sprenkel, note 1 above, at page 114.

21   Jerome A. Cohen, note 3 above, at page 1207.

22   Jerome A. Cohen, note 3 above, at page 1207.

23   Stanley Lubman, note 2 above, at page 1292.

24   See Sybille van der Sprenkel, note 1 above, at page 21: 'The attachment of Chinese people to their village was almost as strong as that to their kin'.

25   Comment by the late Tan Sri Lee Siow Mong, a Malaysian expert on traditional Chinese culture whom I met on 8 July 1982 at Kuala Lumpur.

26   Derk Bodde and Clarence Morris, note 14 above, at pages 5-6.

27   Quoted in Jerome A. Cohen, note 3 above, at page 1215; see also Sybille van der Sprenkel, note 1 above, at page 77. Isabella L. Bird gives a good eye-witness account of a court trial in the Nam

Hooi *Yamen* (or Magistrate's Court) at Guangzhou (formerly Canton) in *THE GOLDEN CHERSONESE and the way thither: Travels In Malaya In 1879*, Oxford University Press, Kuala Lumpur, 1982, at pages 74-79. She describes the *yamen* as a 'chamber of horror'.

28   Jernigan, *China in Law and Commerce* (1905) at page 189 quoted in Jerome A. Cohen, note 3 above, at page 1215.

29   Hu Chang-tu, *China-Its People, Its Society, Its Culture*, Hraf Press, New Haven, 1960, at page 3. See also Kung-Chuan Hsiao, *Compromise in Imperial China*, School of International Studies, University of Washington, Seattle, 1979, at pages 6-8.

30   Stanley Lubman, note 2 above, at pages 1292-1293. He also observes that the gentry status was sometimes acquired by 'purchasing degrees and offices from the State'.

31   Sybille van der Sprenkel, note 1 above, at pages 21-22.

32   Hu Chang-tu, note 29 above, at pages 2-3.

33   Stanley Lubman, note 2 above, at pages 1292-1293.

34   Sybille van der Sprenkel, note 1 above, at page 100; see also Jerome A. Cohen, note 2 above, at page 1218.

35   Sybille van der Sprenkel, note 1 above, at page 119; Stanley Lubman, note 2 above, at page 1299.

36   Term used by Hu Hsien-Chin, quoted in Sybille van der Sprenkel, note 1 above, at page 17. See also Jerome A. Cohen, note 2 above, a t page 1217.

37   Sybille van der Sprenkel, note 1 above, at page 19.

38   Sybille van der Sprenkel, note 1 above, at page 19.

39   On the significance of *ganqing*, see Chapter 3.

40   Stanley Lubman, note 2 above, at page 1294.

41   Stanley Lubman, note 2 above, at pages 1293-1294. See also Jerome A. Cohen, note 2 above, at page 1219.

42   Sybille van der Sprenkel, note 1 above, at page 81; see also Jerome A. Cohen, note 2 above, at page 1216.

43   Jerome A. Cohen, note 2 above, at pages 1216-1217.

44   Chu T'ung-tsu, note 4 above, at page 37.

45   *chia ch'o pu ker wai yang* (phrase translated by the author).

46   Sybille van der Sprenkel, note 1 above, at page 84; Jerome A. Cohen, note 2 above, at pages 1216-1219.

47   Jerome A. Cohen, note 2 above, at pages 1221-1222.

48   Sybille van der Sprenkel, note 1 above, at page 20.

49   Stanley Lubman, note 2 above, at page 1294.

50   Sybille van der Sprenkel, note 1 above, at pages 89-90.

51   Sybille van der Sprenkel, note 1 above, at page 90.

52   Derk Bodde and Clarence Morris, note 14 above, at page 6.

53   Term used by K. S. Latourette, *THE CHINESE, their History and Culture*, Macmillan Company, New York, 1964, at page 469.

54   Comment by the late Tan Sri Lee Siow Mong, note 25 above.

55   Stanley Lubman, note 2 above, at page 1295.

56   Stanley Lubman, note 2 above, at page 1295; K. S. Latourette, note 57 above, at page 469; Sybille van der Sprenkel, note 1 above, at page 69; Jerome A. Cohen, note 2 above, at page 1213.

57   K. S. Latourette, note 57 above, at page 469; Phillip M. Chen, note 8 above, at page 8; Stanley Lubman, note 2 above, at page 1296; Sybille van der Sprenkel, note 1 above, at page 75; ; Jerome A. Cohen, note 2 above, at pages 1213-1214.

58   Comment by the late Tan Sri Lee Siow Mong, note 25 above; also, Sybille van der Sprenkel, note 1 above, at page 138.

59   Sybille van der Sprenkel, note 1 above, at page 138; Stanley Lubman, note 2 above, at page 1296; Jerome A. Cohen, note 2 above, at page 1212.

60   Sybille van der Sprenkel, note 1 above, at pages 70-71; Stanley Lubman, note 2 above, at page 1296; Jerome A. Cohen, note 2 above, at page 1213.

61   Sybille van der Sprenkel, note 1 above, at page 69.

62   Sybille van der Sprenkel, note 1 above, at page 74; Stanley Lubman, note 2 above, at page 1296; Bird, note 27 above, at pages 78-79.

63   Sybille van der Sprenkel, note 1 above, at page 69; Jerome A. Cohen, note 2 above, at page 1214; Bird, note 27 above, at pages 75, 77-79.

64   Sybille van der Sprenkel, note 1 above, at page 69.

65   Bird, note 27 above, at page 69.

66   Bird, note 27 above, at pages 71-72.

67   Sybille van der Sprenkel, note 1 above, at page 69.

68   Sybille van der Sprenkel, note 1 above, at page 69.

69   Sybille van der Sprenkel, note 1 above, at page 69.

70   Comment by the late Tan Sri Lee Siow Mong, note 25 above.

71   See Stanley Lubman, note 2 above, at page 1296; Sybille van der Sprenkel, note 1 above, at page 135; Jerome A. Cohen, note 2 above, at pages 1201, 1212-1215.

72   Phillip M. Chen, note 8 above, at pages 3-4.

73   Stanley Lubman, note 2 above, at page 1297.

74   Stanley Lubman, note 2 above, at page 1297. See also Sybille van der Sprenkel, note 1 above, at page 78.

75   Stanley Lubman, note 2 above, at page 1297.

76   Comment by the late Tan Sri Lee Siow Mong, note 25 above.

77   Simon Roberts, *Order And Dispute: An Introduction To Legal Anthropology*, Penguin Books, Harmondsworth, 1979, at page 67.

78   Stanley Lubman, note 2 above, at page 1298.

79   Sybille van der Sprenkel, note 1 above, at page 117.

80   Sybille van der Sprenkel, note 1 above, at page 117.

81   Sybille van der Sprenkel, note 1 above, at page 116.

82   Stanley Lubman, note 2 above, at page 1297; Jerome A. Cohen, note 2 above, at pages 1216-1222.

83   Sybille van der Sprenkel, note 1 above, at page 84.

84   Sybille van der Sprenkel, note 1 above, at pages 85-86.

85   Sybille van der Sprenkel, note 1 above, at page 88. See also Hu Chang-tu, note 29 above, at page 166. This observation is of relevance to Malaysia because most of the Chinese immigrants originated from these two southern Provinces and as Hu Chang-tu remarks, at page 166, 'the importance of the Fukien and Kwantung Clans is still felt in overseas Chinese communities that have emigrated from these areas'.

86   Hu Chang-tu, note 29 above, at page 166.

87   Stanley Lubman, note 2 above, at page 1298. See also Jerome A. Cohen, note 2 above, at page 1201.

88   An excellent description of the process of mediation is found in M. Yang, *A CHINESE VILLAGE: TAITOU, SHANTUNG PROVINCE 134* (1945), at pages 165-166 which is referred to in Sybille van der Sprenkel, note 1 above, at page 101 and referred to also in Kung-Chuan Hsiao, *Compromise in Imperial China*, School of International Studies, University of Washington, Seattle, 1979, at page 58; Stanley Lubman, note 2 above, at page 1298; Jerome A. Cohen, note 2 above, at page 1220.

89   Sybille van der Sprenkel, note 1 above, at page 101.

90   Kung-Chuan Hsiao, note 88 above, at page 59.

91   Kung-Chuan Hsiao, note 88 above, at page 61.

92   Kung-Chuan Hsiao, note 88 above, at page 59.

93   Kung-Chuan Hsiao, note 88 above, at page 61.

94   On the importance of 'face', see Chapter 3, above.

95   Sybille van der Sprenkel, note 1 above, at page 115.

96   Sybille van der Sprenkel, note 1 above, at page 115.

97   Kung-Chuan Hsiao, note 88 above, at pages 58-59.

98   Author of *The Fabric of Chinese Society* , New York, 1953, quoted in Sybille van der Sprenkel, note 1 above, at page 101.

99   A strong, yet suitable, adjective used by Sybille van der Sprenkel, see Sybille van der Sprenkel, note 1 above, at page 102.

100   Stanley Lubman, note 2 above, at page 1298.

101   Stanley Lubman, note 2 above, at page 1298. See also Sybille van der Sprenkel, note 1 above, at pages 85 and 92.

102   Jerome A. Cohen, note 2 above, at page 1201; Stanley Lubman, note 2 above, at page 1298.

103   Kung-Chuan Hsiao, note 88 above, at page 62.

104   Stanley Lubman, note 2 above, at page 1299.

105   Stanley Lubman, note 2 above, at page 1299; Sybille van der Sprenkel, note 1 above, at page 119.

106   Sybille van der Sprenkel, note 1 above, at page 108. See also E. N. Anderson and Marja L. Anderson, *Fishing In Troubled Waters: Research On The Chinese Fishing Industry In West Malaysia*, The Orient Cultural Service, Taipei, 1977, at page 106.

107   Kung-Chuan Hsiao, note 88 above, at page 62.

108   Sybille van der Sprenkel, note 1 above, at pages 119-120; Stanley Lubman, note 2 above, at page 1299; Jerome A. Cohen, note 2 above, at page 1224; Kung-Chuan hsiao, note 88 above, at page 67.

109   Kung-Chuan Hsiao, note 88 above, at page 62.

110   Sybille van der Sprenkel, note 1 above, at page 119.

111   Yang (1945) attempts to show that public opinion was a powerful sanction at page 150, quoted in Sybille van der Sprenkel, note 1 above, at page 98 and in Stanley Lubman, note 2 above, at page 1299.

112   Sybille van der Sprenkel, note 1 above, at page 120; Stanley Lubman, note 2 above, at page 1299.

113   Kung-chuan Hsiao, note 88 above, at page 67.

114   Jerome A. Cohen, note 2 above, at page 1208.

115   Stanley Lubman, note 2 above, at page 1300; Jerome A. Cohen, note 2 above, at page 1225. For a list of virtues of mediation practised in contemporary China, see Donald C. Clarke, 'Dispute Resolution In China' (1991) 5 *Journal of Chinese Law* 245, at page 271.

116   Jerome A. Cohen, note 2 above, at page 1219.

117   Sybille van der Sprenkel, note 1 above, at page 129.

5 Society, Law and Justice Among Rural Chinese Malaysians

It is better to die of starvation than to become a thief; it is better to be vexed to death than to bring a lawsuit.[1]

Introduction

'What is a lawyer?' was the question my very traditional-minded late grandmother posed to me when I became a first year Law undergraduate at the University of Malaya, Kuala Lumpur, in May 1979. To my surprise, I found it hard to explain to her, grasping for some equivalent expression in Hokkien. Due to this, I later realised that in ancient China, no 'lawyer' had existed and consequently, there was no Hokkien equivalent of such a word.[2]

To most rural Chinese Malaysians, the lawyer is viewed as an alien being, preferably to be avoided and not to be befriended. Proximity to a lawyer, especially in a professional context, arouses village suspicion that there is some kind of trouble. Usually, there is no need for calling on a lawyer's assistance due to the fact that, in private matters, most rural Chinese Malaysians adhere to family principles whereby the family rules operate effectively as strong social sanctions in the resolution of disputes. In the event that the family elders cannot resolve them, the local community leaders may be approached. As such, self-help in disputing behaviour seems to be the social norm.

In criminal matters, the mediators may advise the disputants to refer them to official authorities, such as the *Penghulu* (or head of the village), the *Ketua Mesyuarat* (or head of the Local Council), the local parliamentary representatives, or the police.

I conducted field interviews, represented in this Chapter as the select case studies, in two rural Chinese villages, Paloh and Tangkak, in the State of Johore in Malaysia nearly two decades ago. No doubt, I have had a continuing interest in the aspect of social change in these places in the intervening period. Therefore, I have sought to make enquiries from relevant respondents regarding the traditional ideas of non-litigiousness and the practice of mediation in settling disputes. In consequence, I have been informed that the cultural tendency to mediate still represents the prevailing norm in Paloh and Tangkak. The traditional attitude of conflict avoidance coupled with the instinctive desire to uphold village harmony continues to be at play. Paloh and Tangkak were selected for field research on the basis of my links: the former, natal, and the latter, adoptive. I was born and bred in Paloh and lived there for a substantial part of my formative years. My parents later moved to Tangkak as a result of their work transfer and we maintained two homes, one in each place. I used to shuttle between the two frequently. To this day, my natal family has maintained close ties with these two places, more so in Paloh where we still own our original place of residence. In fact, my father is well-regarded as a local influential leader, being the Chairman of the Hokkien Eng Choon Association. He is a clan chief, so to speak.

The field research was done on the basis of participant observation. Interviews were conducted with a cross-section of the rural Chinese Malaysian communities of Paloh and Tangkak, ranging from housewives, students, teachers, businessmen, officials to outstanding village leaders and clan association chiefs. The assertions made in this Chapter have, in a sense, withstood the test of time to a large extent. As mentioned earlier, I have continually sought views in recent years on these village communities to revise my findings. However, tradition dies hard. Sociologically, this seems more so in the case of the Chinese where the norms of tradition, stability and constancy continue to enjoy a mainstay. But, it would be erroneous to think that village society has remained static. Certainly, the influences of modern lifestyles, the increase in commercial relationships in village life, and the availability of better economic opportunities elsewhere have contributed to social changes among such village folk. Nevertheless, by and large, with regard to disputing behaviour, these rural Chinese are still far more inclined towards the informal means of dispute settlement, i.e.

mediation, and reliant upon the operation of social sanctions in minimizing friction in everyday life.

In recent times, there have been two major social changes recorded in these villages. Firstly, the referral of disputes mainly to the local parliamentarians for mediation in preference to clan chiefs as modern village life is more bound up with the bureaucracy. Pertinently, these local parliamentarians who are elected representatives are also of Chinese ethnic background with whom the villagers share a common tie. In the collectivist context, these parliamentarians are the members of the in-group who are respected and trusted by village folk. Secondly, the increase of contractual relationships in village life has necessitated somewhat more formal procedures in dealing with contract disputes, with some inevitably ending in litigation. The likelihood of litigation is, therefore, seen to be comparatively on the rise. Despite such discernible social changes, the truth of the matter is that mediation continues to prevail over litigation, village life is more concerned with harmony and the cultural trait of non-litigiousness continues to be relevant.

Interestingly, traditional Chinese mediation is alive and well not just among rural Chinese Malaysians, but evident among rural Chinese folk in various parts of the globe. Research undertaken in the past has reached the same theme of the traditional non-litigiousness of the Chinese and their tendency to mediate. Such studies have included rural communities in the People's Republic of China, Taiwan, Thailand, to name a few.[3]

The Chinese Malaysian Saga

Popular folklore has always been the delight of the old and young alike. Bred in a rural environment, I had been accustomed to the many favourite stories untiringly told and retold by my late grandmother in the evenings, or as bedtime stories. My young mind then did not realise that I was unwittingly registering the history of a great culture. To me, such stories came closer to legends than as real-life events. But, I would be chided by my late grandmother, who would then go at length to make me appreciate their significance.

Much of the knowledge of the Chinese ancestry is passed down this way. My late grandparents originated from the Province of Fukien in South China. My late grandfather came to Malaya (as it was then known) and saw for himself the rich hinterland in which to build a new home. He then sent for my late grandmother who was, at that time, in her twenties. There was at that time in China widespread famine and disease, much poverty and political unrest. That was at the beginning of the twentieth century.

History writers such as Purcell, Turnbull and Comber who were interested in the history of the Malay Peninsula have invariably dwelt on the topic of Chinese immigration. Reading their books reminded me of some of my late grandmother's stories. They were true after all.

Although historical records show that Chinese contacts with the Malay Peninsula began as early as the fifth century,[4] substantial Chinese immigration did not take place until about the middle of the nineteenth century. As Dr Yap points out, 'people emigrate for many reasons: for love of adventure, the necessity to escape persecution and to seek a safe haven, or the desire to discover new opportunities and a better life or new worlds to conquer'.[5] With regard to Chinese exodus, however, the real reasons can be attributed to the unendurable life of the peasantry in the Southern Chinese Provinces, natural calamities, the pressure of over-population and political upheaval. Purcell observes that the reason why many overseas Chinese in Malaysia are of Hokkien or Cantonese origin may be due to the 'geographic contiguity'[6] of Malaysia in relation to these South-eastern Chinese Provinces. Another explanation is that the main trading ports of Guangdong and Fukien – Canton (Guangchow), Swatow and Amoy – had already established contacts with the outside world and it is, therefore, not surprising for the inhabitants to eventually find their way to the then Straits Settlements of Penang, Singapore and Malaya.[7]

Of course, this exodus would not have been the way it was had it not been for the attractions of the Malay Peninsula. The rich tin fields of Larut and Selangor in the nineteenth century held great promise. The beginning of the twentieth century witnessed the meteoric boom of the rubber industry. Chinese labour was in demand.[8] The Chinese were prepared to work hard. In fact, the Chinese are reputed to be a people of great industry.[9] The Chinese who arrived in Malaya were first known as the *sinkeh*, or new visitors. The men folk were the ones who ventured without their women folk. It was thought that the men would accumulate wealth and then eventually return to China, with no intention of a permanent settlement in the new land. Most Chinese, bound by the duty of ancestral worship (tied to the Confucian tenet of *hsiao*), disliked the idea of emigration, unless compelled by dire necessity. And, with respect to the pioneer immigrants, the majority of them would prefer to return to China to die.[10]

The early immigrants fell into two categories: those who were able to pay for their passage and the indentured labourers. The former were the more fortunate ones who already had some relatives or clansmen on whom they could depend for a while. The latter had to enter into a sort of bondage with their masters in return for free passage. This was known as the *sin-kueh* system, or popularly regarded as the 'coolie trade'.[11] Vaughan describes the coolie trade in the following vivid terms:

> A number of Chinese familiar with the Straits collect them [immigrants] in China by holding out prospects of a speedy fortune and quick return to their native land and bring them down in junks, sailing vessels, or steamers, and dispose of them to the residents to the best advantage, the immigrants mortgaging their labour for twelve months to repay their passage money'.[12]

It is common knowledge that this coolie trade was fraught with abuse. The collecting-agents for Chinese labourers were provided handsomely with a capitation fee for every emigrant they brought to the port of departure in China to be sailed to the Malay Peninsula. The unsuspecting fellow-countrymen were easily entrapped. Their sea-journey was horrendous: they were often herded into crammed and overloaded vessels. Needless to say, mortality rate was high. Their common method of protesting against oppression was by taking their own lives.[13] For those who finally reached their destination, they were anxiously awaited by their would-be masters. Most were quickly taken to toil in the pepper and gambier farms while others were also swiftly engaged to work in the mines owned by Malay territorial chiefs.[14] Vaughan points out that 'sometimes the coolies were disposed of according to their qualifications: a master workman fetching a high price, a labourer something less, and a sickly man a few dollars'.[15] Some of such immigrants who had not yet been disposed of were kept and detained on board or in specially-hired lodging houses. Many eventually fell victim to the wretched conditions and the unaccustomed malarial environment.[16]

The then British Colonial Government encouraged Chinese immigration as this was a means of obtaining cheap labour. The industriousness of the Chinese was a great asset in helping to open up new lands for agriculture or for mining. There were no immigration laws to restrict or control the influx. It was not until 1914 that indentured labour was abolished, and it was not until 1930, with the introduction of the Immigration Restriction Ordinance, that completely free immigration came under surveillance. This Ordinance was effective for four years after which it was superseded by the Aliens Ordinance on 1 April 1933. The Chinese immigrants, being substantial in number, were the most affected by these laws.[17]

Subsequently, the Japanese Occupation of Malaya (1941-1945) put a stop to further immigration.

Currently, the Chinese in Malaysia form the second largest ethnic group, with the majority of them living in the urban areas.

Traditional Values, Customs and The New Land

It will be hard to understand why most Chinese Malaysians behave the way they do without a preliminary insight into their traditional culture and lifestyle.[18] As is well-commented upon, 'tradition persists into the present, and long-established patterns of ancient society are reflected in contemporary behaviour'.[19] The present, therefore, cannot be adequately understood without making reference to the past.

It is not possible to delve upon every aspect of traditional Chinese culture. Suffice it to say that rural Chinese Malaysians generally continue to observe the main traditional customs, rites and rituals, as exemplified below. More relevantly, it is such observances which point to the fact that the preservation of such values continue to make an impact on their views on society, law and justice and maintain a role in their legal thinking.

The newcomer to Chinese culture is almost always beguiled by the variety of customs practised by the people who boast a great civilization behind them. Some of these customs have been practised with modification by the Chinese in different provinces in China as well as in their respective adoptive countries.[20] Most rural Chinese Malaysian communities are primarily reliant on agriculture and, as such, their way of life appears not to differ drastically from the life of the peasantry in traditional China. There is, thus, good cause for transmitting customary practices and traditional values to the ensuing generations. Moreover, as Dr Yap points out, the Chinese immigrants were much concerned with their children's education, something which had been deprived them during their hard lives in traditional China.[21] Chinese education is more popular in rural communities where the environment continues to facilitate the inculcation and perpetuation of traditional Chinese (Confucian) values and where such values can continue to be practised in a meaningful context.

In contrast with urban Chinese Malaysians, urban societies are characteristically more complex, anonymous and metropolitan. The urban Chinese Malaysians would, therefore, find it relatively hard to adhere to their traditional customs when their everyday lives involve constant intermingling with other Malaysian races like the Malays and the Indians. Urban Chinese are more encouraged to be assimilated in a Malaysian society. Above all, there is a conscious choice in educating their children in mainstream Malay schools where the Malay language is regarded as 'the language of educational advancement and job opportunity'.[22] It follows, as a matter of consequence, that a rejection of one's own language is a handicap in understanding one's own culture properly.

Chinese customs can best be seen within the context of the celebration or observance of events or festivals.[23] And the Chinese have a great number of occasions or festive seasons diligently observed year after year. Festivity, an occasion for rejoicing, is also an occasion to worship the ancestors in accordance with the Confucian tradition. The proper person to conduct the ritual and the ceremony is the son. Sumptuous food is proffered to appease the spirits of the ancestors, together with the burning of sacred paper-money in their honour as the prayers are uttered.[24] When the burnt sacred paper-money turns to ash, the son has to return to the ancestral altar to continue with the prayers. The way to find out if the ancestral spirits have been appeased is by tossing two coins. If the tossed coins show a head and a tail, it means that the ancestral spirits have been propitiated. If not, the tossing will repeatedly continue until the coins produce the desired result.[25] Once propitiated, the food offerings can then be cleared from the altar, leaving only the incense to continue to be burnt in honour of the ancestors.[26]

Ancestral worship plays a central and indispensable role in traditional Chinese life. This is lucidly explained as follows:

'Ancestor worship' has a practical and utilitarian as well as a religious or spiritual aspect, and is consciously and deliberately maintained as a method whereby a Chinese family not only shows its reverence or respect for its departed forefathers but also maintains the continuity of its traditions, strengthens its ties with its scattered members and collateral branches, and safeguards the material interests of its descendants. In actual practice, the cult is not so much a cult of ancestors as a cult of the family.[27]

The practice of ancestral worship, therefore, is reminiscent of the Chinese belief in the inter-connectedness between the material world and the spiritual world. Such an inter-dependent worldview underlines the meaning of relationships and the significance of harmony: cosmologically between Nature and Humanity, between the dead and the living, and practically between the living and the living.[28] In other words, ancestral worship symbolically links the relationships between the spiritual and the human worlds, and help to maintain close family bonds by bringing the existing family members together in prayers and feasting. Such an observance of customs continually reminds the Chinese of the value of inter-personal harmony, which, in turn, impacts upon their attitude towards disputing behaviour. There is, therefore, a constant desire to maintain village harmony, and a natural instinct to stay away from inter-personal conflicts.

Below is a survey of the salient Chinese customs which are practised to this day.

Birth

For the Chinese, birth has always been an occasion to rejoice. This is especially so when the newborn is a male. To the Westerner, this attitude may be discriminatory. But, as we have examined, a male heir bears important social consequences in traditional Chinese society: he is the one to preserve and perpetuate family lineage and perform the ancestral rites.[29] As such, when a mother gives birth to a boy, she is surrounded by well-wishing village folk who come to praise and congratulate the family for their 'good life', i.e. their fortune in begetting a son.

The real pomp and pageantry occurs at the conclusion of the first lunar month since birth. This is also known as the 'full-moon' ceremony. The ceremony involves relatives and close family friends gathering together in the household to celebrate the occasion. Gifts, usually in the form of jewellery, are given to wish the baby and his family plenty of fortune, health and wealth. The giving of 'gold' jewellery is thus symbolic.

Naming is a prerogative of the family elders. In my own family, my late grandfather was responsible for naming us. Names are often chosen after great deliberation. In some Chinese families, lineage requires all the children to carry a common name, placed in the middle or at the end of the given name, in order to identify particular generations.[30] The male baby is often given a name which suggests brilliance, scholarliness, greatness, strength, loyalty and so on. The female baby is given names which project feminine qualities like beauty, love or gentleness. It is generally believed that a child who bears a name with special meanings will exhibit those characteristics in adulthood.

Sometimes, two names are assumed by the child. This happens in two cases:

1. A Chinese is normally said to have a personal name used in the family and a personal name used in school (or society). The one used in the family could be given due to superstition. It is sometimes feared that a baby is not supposed to own a name or it may attract the evil spirits. The family elders will commonly use the name of an animal when addressing the child at home. 'Ah Kow', meaning dog, or 'Ah The'r', meaning pig, are the usual ones employed. A school-name is necessary as the child attains school-going age and a careful selection is made to enable the child to achieve the inherent qualities of the name.

2. It may happen that a name given to a child is for dual purposes: family and society. However, the Chinese are generally rather superstitious. An anxious parent may go to the Chinese temple or a fortune-teller to ask if a correct name has been given to the child. If the answer is in the negative, a new name may have to be selected. It is also pertinent to note that the Chinese believe that the human body is composed of five elements: metal, wood, water, earth and fire. If a child is believed to be deficient in a particular element, the parent will alter the child's name to incorporate that element in his or her name.

Marriage

Marriage, for the Chinese, is another joyous occasion. In accordance with their collectivist nature, the wedding guests are usually those of the parents' rather than the bridal couple's. Chinese marriage is, therefore, more of a public than a private affair. Chinese marriages are believed to be made in Heaven.[31] In the Confucianist view, a marriage is regarded as a bond between two families.[32] In traditional Chinese culture, marriage is, therefore, more functional than romantic. It is the duty of the parents of the bridal couple to ensure continual lineage. An important aspect of this lies in the perpetuation of ancestral worship.

Most traditional Chinese marriages are preceded by a reference to the Chinese horoscope (based on animal years) and other spiritual indicators (for example, oracular consultations at Chinese temples) to predict the success or otherwise of a matrimonial union. Apparently, such consultations will reveal the compatibility of the couple. The most common practice involves a study of the 'Eight-Character' between the bridal couple. The Eight-Character is derived from the hour, day, month and year of birth. If the character turns out to be incompatible, the engagement is cancelled.[33]

It is also customary for the bridegroom to provide a sum of money known as the bride-wealth to the bride's family to enable the bride to make some initial purchase. The bride's family cannot retain any part of the bride-wealth. In some instances, through the consent of the bride's parents, the bride-wealth may be dispensed with.[34]

Wedding banquets are customary. This is an occasion to invite families and friends to feast and to cement their relationships. The bride and bridegroom usually offer tea to the family elders as a sign of respect. Ancestral worship is also part and parcel of the occasion.

Funerals

Death is not only unwelcome in traditional Chinese culture, it is also a highly taboo subject and much associated with ill fortune.

In accordance with Confucian tradition, the observance of filial piety in relation to a funeral is paramount.[35] The eldest son takes charge of the conduct of the funeral and performs the requisite rites. He is also expected to carry out a lifetime of ancestral worship. This is consonant with the Confucian precept of *hsiao* inherent in *li*.[36]

In village life, funerals are communal events in the sense that most villagers assist the grieving family in the rites and rituals, and in cooking meals for the family and the sympathisers.

Chinese New Year Festival

The origin of Chinese New Year is legendary. It is based on the lunar calendar and denotes the passing of time in terms of a twelve-year cycle. These twelve years are represented by the twelve animals in the following order: rat, ox, tiger, rabbit, dragon, snake, horse, sheep, monkey, rooster, dog and pig.[37] Each animal, in a particular year, is said to bear one of the five elements of metal, wood, water, earth and fire. Consequently, each animal cycle takes sixty years to complete.

The Chinese New Year festival is by far the most celebrated event. In China, it is known as the Spring Festival. The celebration is marked by the family reunion dinner held on the eve of the New Year, and goes on for fifteen days, with the significant ones being the first day to the fifth day, the ninth day (for the Hokkiens), and the fifteenth day which is 'Chap Go Meh'.

Because of the Chinese fervent belief in luck, the first day of the Festival is fraught with taboos. For instance, brooms must not be seen lest good luck for the year is swept away. Porcelain and breakable items must be handled with care as any breakage spells bad luck.[38]

As usual, prayers are offered to one's ancestors before the family partakes of the food. In village life, it is common to exchange gifts, usually in the form of food hampers. There is again feasting involved.

Ching-Ming

This is the Chinese equivalent of 'All Souls' Day'. It is observed at any time during the first half of the third lunar month. This is the time when the graves of the relatives are visited and cleaned, and it also entails sacrificial offerings.

This custom reinforces the practice of ancestral worship, based on the Confucian notion of filial piety. It is a day when the living commemorate their dead. It also provides another opportunity to bring family members, near and far, together and remind them of the importance of family relationships.[39]

Dumpling Festival

This Festival is said to be linked to the suicidal death of a patriotic poet-minister who sacrificed his own life in order to escape the evil practices of a corrupt government.[40] Legend has it that Ch'u Yuan, a great poet and a minister of the State of Ch'u became disillusioned with the corrupt government of the day. He was subsequently dismissed through palace intrigue and preferred a death of honour rather than to be a corrupt minister himself. He was believed to have clasped a huge stone and jumped into the sea in an act of patriotism. Fearing that his body might be eaten by the fish, sympathisers prepared dumplings made of glutinous rice and threw them into the sea as fish food in the hope of luring the fish away from him.[41]

This Festival is celebrated on the fifth day of the fifth lunar month. It symbolises Chinese insistence on the virtues of integrity, loyalty and patriotism in governance.

This Festival has been popularised as the Dragon Boat Festival, as can be seen with the holding of dragon boat races in various parts of the world including Malaysia, Singapore, Hong Kong, and Australia.

Hungry Ghosts' Festival

As noted before, the Chinese believe in the inter-dependence between the material and the spiritual worlds. Thus, the welfare of the spirits is linked to the welfare of human beings on earth. The well-being of the human world is a favour granted by Heaven pleased with human behaviour. It is also believed that there may be some wandering spirits who may have been forgotten or neglected by their living relatives. The hungry ghosts are 'the category of neglected shades, who have not been cared for by their living relatives and who are, therefore, prone to be malignant and mischievous'.[42]

The Hungry Ghosts' Festival is observed during the whole of the seventh lunar month, a time, so it is believed, when these spirits are released from Hell.[43] Among the very conservative and superstitious, the fear that these wandering spirits may disturb the living is a real fear indeed. As Vaughan puts it, 'during this month the spirits are supposed to wander about the earth and if not propitiated plague the offenders with divers, pains and aches and more serious mishaps'.[44]

This period of observance acts as a reminder of the importance of observing filial piety by carrying on ancestral worship. Food is an important theme, as is the case with all Chinese festivities. And, food is a bonding agent in Chinese relationships.

For the commercial world, it may be helpful to note that this is the month when one finds a reluctance by the Chinese to engage in business activities as it is considered a very inauspicious period. For instance, there are generally no weddings scheduled during this period, and restaurant banquets suffer a decline as such. Business people also consciously refrain from entering into contracts, commencing new ventures or engaging in negotiations. This is out of a fear of attracting bad luck.

Mooncake Festival

The true origin of the Mooncake Festival remains unascertained.[45] It is celebrated on the fifteenth day of the eighth lunar month, and is also known as the Mid-Autumn Festival.

The celebration is marked by an exchange of gifts of mooncakes of a variety of flavours. It is yet another opportunity to foster inter-personal ties. It also reflects the relationship between the Moon (Nature) and Humanity, and the importance of observing harmony. Festive rejoicing is the hallmark. As expected, it provides another occasion for ancestral worship.[46]

In modern times, this Festival is delightfully seen by a colourful display of lanterns. Thus, it is also called the Lantern Festival.

Winter Festival

This is the last of the festivals observed during the year, and occurs during the final month of the lunar year. It started with the old agrarian communities in China who rested during the cold winter, and who waited for spring to plant their crops again.[47]

As usual, the Festival serves as an occasion to perform ancestral worship. Specially-made sweet and colourful marble-shaped rice-balls are served. The round shape is to signify family unity. It is generally believed that everyone is older by a year during this Festival.

The above customary practices, passed down from bygone times, point to the continual cultural emphasis on establishing and preserving relationships, in aid of promoting social harmony. It may be said that modern generations may continue to practise them without realizing their original meaning or significance. However, the fact that they are practised serves the purpose of bonding family members and friends. The corollary of such a close kinship is to remind each other of their specific social roles, to uphold harmony, and, as far as possible, to keep disputes at bay.

Traditional Attitudes Towards Law: A Perpetuation

'The Chinese in Tangkak,' said Mr Wu Tien Hwa,[48] a former Tangkak *Ketua Mesyuarat* (Head of the Local Council), 'still retain many traditional values and practices'. 'The rural Chinese here still observe tradition', echoed another respondent, Mr Tee Seng Meng, a retired Chinese school-teacher in Tangkak. In another instance, Mr Lee Seok Yew, a retired teacher from Paloh Chinese School asserted that, 'Law is only one of the many ways of solving problems. However, the manner in which it solves problems is destructive, not constructive. Villagers here observe *li* and thus there is no need for them to resort to the law courts to settle their problems. Most of them rely on *ganqing* and settle their disputes through mediation'.[49]

All the respondents interviewed invariably agree that the formal law comes into play largely in criminal matters, for instance, in cases of murder, robbery and grievous hurt. In civil matters, the disputes are amicably settled out of court. As one respondent aptly puts it, 'the Chinese people are normally afraid of an involvement with the law. To get involved with the law necessarily implies the loss of finance, time and reputation. It is easier to approach a person in the same village in whom the disputant can place his confidence, his trust and psychological reliance for help'.[50]

The Chinese are also traditionalists by nature and prefer to adopt the proverbial Chinese conservative attitude of 'what was good enough for my ancestors is good enough for me'.[51] Change occurs very slowly. The average rural Chinese Malaysian is conservative in outlook where superstition maintains a viable role.[52]

Goh Bee Keong stated that the role of the law was to maintain peace and order in society but for the Chinese in general, there was also the belief that 'let disputes become small, and let small disputes be reduced to none' which implied that the law played a limited role in a Chinese community since other social factors were more important. Such other social factors, as explored in Chapter 3, are the concern for face, the preservation of *ganqing* (good relations), the cultivation of *renqing* (personal goodwill), the virtue of *rang* (yielding), and the family rule of *hsiao* (filial piety).[53]

'There is no room for the law to operate if all fellow humans act morally towards one another and treat each other like brothers and sisters', said the late Madam Tan Sok.[54] During her lifetime, she firmly believed in the principle of harmony as the prime governing factor in human relationships.

In a rural Chinese community, the members are all too often eager to maintain 'face'. If any dispute arises, it is better to submerge any undue publicity. To this end, the disputants often agree to settle their dispute which is a 'quiet' and expeditious way of terminating it. In some cases, this may amount to dispute suppression. Private matters relating to internal family disputes, quarrels with neighbours, land boundary disputes, community misunderstandings, are often settled amicably amongst the disputants by reference of the conflict to an independent and well-respected mediator.[55] To resort to the courts would destroy *ganqing* between the parties and make their continuing face-to-face daily living unbearable. In village life, the principle of harmony continues to be regarded as crucial since there exists inter-dependence, and village setting provides for communal interests to take precedence over individual concerns.

Access To Justice

Dispute settlement appears to be the predominant mode of obtaining access to justice. Mr Wu Tien Hwa remarked that tradition died hard in Tangkak. It can be seen that control of the family lies in the *chia chang* (or head of the family) who exercises considerable power over the members within it. The concept of *tsu* (clan) is still very strong, making people with a common surname readily group together.

The philosophy of observing social harmony is a prevalent concept among rural Chinese folk. Very commonly, a respected village head or any respectable representative capable of gaining the confidence, respect and trust of the disputing parties will be invited to 'adjudicate' on the matter in question. Such a representative in modern village life these days may include the local parliamentarians. Life in the village community is comparatively simple and many 'coffee-shop lawyers' can easily be spotted. These 'coffee-shop lawyers' are the persons who are fond of gratuitously offering advice to the disputing parties by basing their argument on the common perception of righteousness. They spread the 'peer wisdom', so to speak. Usually, this system works as the villagers' disputes are localized in nature.

Apart from the village headman, there is the clan chief who mediates between disputing parties. The clan chief - who is often a revered person with a high social standing and may be of sound economic position - is the one who mediates between disputing clan groups, who enters into negotiations and who acts as an independent, objective go-between. Clan associations can be of two types - one consisting of people bearing a common surname, the other comprising people of the same dialect group. In Tangkak, the more active clan associations are the Hokkien Eng Choon Association, the Kwang Sou Association and the Teochew Association. In Paloh, the Hokkien Eng Choon Association is seen as active and influential.

The principle by which the dispute settlers base their decision is essentially that of common reason, in order to seek a compromise solution between the disputants. Normally, during the negotiations, the unreasonable party is supposed to listen to reason and to accept the outcome of the negotiation process graciously. The aggrieved party will also be advised to concede a little so that a compromise can be made.

When mediation is successful, the remedies are many and varied. For trivial matters, the unreasonable party will be made to offer 'mediating tea' to the wronged party and both will shake hands to restore the bond of fraternity.

Sometimes, the clan associations concerned will help organize a dinner to invite the relatives and close friends of both parties where all ill-feelings will be deemed to have vanished from the parties concerned.

The modern method gaining popularity nowadays is publication of a public apology in the local Chinese newspaper. This method is resorted to when the disputants cannot agree on the choice of, or do not wish to consult a mediator, or when the offended party insists on a public apology to restore his 'face' and redeem his otherwise tarnished reputation.

Usually, if a dispute involves defamation, it is considered to be rather serious. If the wronged party succeeds in the negotiation, he or she will invariably demand a piece of red cloth and a pair of red candles.[56] The significance of the red cloth, culturally, is to bring happiness back to the family, that 'good things are yet to be'. The red candles are to be lit on the ancestral mantelpiece. Within the Chinese community, when a person is defamed, it means the reputation of the whole family and the whole line of ancestry before him or her is at stake. Therefore, the significance of the red candles is to inform the ancestors that 'I have retrieved your good name which you have so carefully built up'. The point to note here is that when the successful 'plaintiff' demands the red cloth and the red candles as a form of remedy, such a demand is regarded as the highest demand and is made when the dispute constitutes a grave matter. This is in line with the Chinese consciously up-keeping their social prestige which they have constantly to live up to in order to maintain 'face' in public.

The following represents a typical traditional mediation process described in conjunction with a mainland Chinese village, which largely echoes the procedure for rural Chinese Malaysians:

> The general procedure is as follows: First, the invited or self-appointed village leaders come to the involved parties to find out the real issues at stake, and also to collect opinions from other villagers concerning the background of the matter. Then they evaluate the case according to their past experience and propose a solution. In bringing the two parties to accept the proposal, the peacemakers have to go back and forth until the opponents are willing to meet half-way. Then a formal party is held either in the village or in the market town, to which are invited the mediators, the village leaders, clan heads, and the heads of the two disputing families. The main feature of such a party is a feast. While it is in progress, the talk may concern anything except the conflict. The expenses of the feast will either be equally shared by the disputing parties or borne entirely by one of

them. If the controversy is settled in a form of 'negotiated peace', that is, if both parties admit their mistakes, the expenses will be equally shared. If the settlement reached shows that only one party was at fault, the expenses are paid by the guilty family. If one party chooses voluntarily, or is forced, to concede to the other... it will assume the entire cost. When the heads or representatives of the disputing families are ushered to the feast, they greet each other and exchange a few words. After a little while they will ask to be excused and depart. Thus, the conflict is settled. [57]

As a matter of course, there will be times when mediation is not possible because the nature of the dispute dictates otherwise. This commonly involves breaches of promise in instances where there are no witnesses. For example, in the case of an outstanding debt, supposing the debtor has already repaid the creditor but the creditor denies the fact and there are no witnesses to testify to the good faith of the debtor, mediation becomes difficult because the mediator will not know who to believe. In instances like this, there is a traditionally grave and serious method that the parties can resort to, i.e. the cutting of a white chicken's head which is symbolic of supernatural judgment. The symbol of the white chicken is the symbol of innocence. By sacrificing the chicken before God, the accused party is in fact telling God that the white chicken is dying - and has to die - on his or her behalf to prove his or her innocence. The cutting of the white chicken's head is accompanied by an oath solemnly conducted, and deadly - in the sense that if the accused party is actually guilty, the chicken has been sacrificed for nothing and he or she must, therefore, face the consequences of arousing the wrath of Heaven. It is believed that the ill consequences would be with the family for generations to follow.

This method of settling disputes - the cutting of a white chicken's head - is considered to be very undesirable in the eyes of the Chinese community. In other words, there is no eye-witness to the event in question. It is beyond human power to attest to the truth of the matter, and. therefore, both parties have decided on the power of God and the Heavens to pass judgment. The consequence is that if the accused party is in fact guilty but has nevertheless taken up the challenge to prove himself or herself, he or she will incur the wrath of the Heavens and will stand to be judged by God. Normally, the guilty would not favour this method. If at all resorted to, this is a method practised by the Taoists since the Buddhists do not believe in taking any form of life. In modern times, this practice is relatively unheard of, but when I was a child in Paloh, a neighbourhood dispute involved the challenge of cutting a white chicken's head as proof of innocence. As events later turned out, the challenge was not taken but the seriousness of the dispute was publicly noted.

In terms of remedies, unlike in a Common Law Justice system where monetary damages are the principal relief sought, very rarely does a disputant in a Chinese dispute settlement process ask for monetary compensation unless the subject matter in dispute is one relating to debt collection, or arrears of rent, or medical expenses in cases where physical hurt is caused. This is consonant with the concept of yielding and compromise as advanced by Confucian ethics. So long as social harmony is achieved, the disputing parties ought not to go beyond the scope of the matter in question. Besides, according to the Confucian view, 'the moral man is a peacemaker, not a litigation maker. Justice is, therefore, associated, not with rights and duties, but with righteousness'.[58] In this way, the disputants and the witnesses as well as the mediators work within prescribed 'legal' and moral rules. The community generally is sensitized to the dispute in question and the principle foremost on every component member's mind is that the break-up of the village is bad, and undesirable.[59]

Often, when dispute procedures fail and the disputing parties do not wish to present their case in a formal court of law, their other alternative may be to invoke the power of the official authorities by going to the government-appointed headmen who may be ethnic Malays. Intermediaries like the community elders are then normally approached by the disputants to intercede on their behalf when requesting official intervention. This is attributable to both the cultural and language barriers.

In other cases, disputants may even resort to powerful secret society members where judgment will be obeyed from fear of the consequences.[60] Secret societies are notorious amongst Chinese communities. They are steeped in rituals and abide by their own code of conduct.

According to a respondent,[61] the secret societies are normally approached for help in the following ways:

1.   If the aggrieved party is a member, he then goes directly to his own secret society to get help from his 'brothers';

2.   If the aggrieved party is a relative of a member of a particular secret society, he can refer his grievance to that member who will in turn 'recommend' his case to the society;

3.   If the aggrieved party has a friend who is a secret society member, the latter may also 'recommend' his case to the society.

The reason why 'recommendation' is necessary is because the secret societies do not simply accept any 'case' for fear of police detection. After all, such societies are outlaws.[62]

There are two distinct classes in every secret society, the Reds and the Whites. The Whites are the non-fighting members whose activities are more insidious. They normally give advice, seek financial aid and attempt to maintain good relationships with the formal law enforcing bodies such as the police. On the other hand, the Reds are the fighting members. When the Whites fail in their negotiation, the Reds will use violence on the opposing party. An outsider can easily identify a Red, but not a White.

In my opinion, the continued existence of the secret societies is unwarranted. Although they claim to protect the rights of the under-privileged, their existence is by its very nature illegal and their operations are violent and untoward. For instance, in their faction rivalries, they often resort to mutual killings and disturb the public peace. As contrasted with the village headmen and clan chiefs whose method of dispute settlement is peaceful and beneficial to all the parties concerned, the secret societies triumph with violence and aggression. In the ultimate analysis, they represent a form of social cancer and their activities should be discontinued.

Case Studies

The following is a collection of select cases solved by means of mediation. The cases cited were mediated by Mr Teong Boon Cheow, the Honorary Life Chairman of the Hokkien Eng Choon Association in Tangkak, and the late Madam Tan Sok, a woman of extraordinary character and leadership whose advice was much sought after when she was resident in Labis (in the 1920s) and Paloh (early 1950s to 1978).

These field studies offer interesting insights on how traditional mediation was conducted. One witnesses the fact that the end result is always a compromise solution, the prevailing norm being social harmony. Other characteristic features which continue to this day are: the informal and intuitive process of mediation, the lack of a formalized and structured approach as found in modern Western mediation, the presence of social pressures which obligates the disputants to mediate, the unique binary (private-public) role played by the mediators, and the appeal to common reason and communal values rather than a reference to the formal law and rules by the mediators in the settlement of disputes. In short, traditional Chinese mediation tends to be, overall, more affective than cognitive. It is also interesting to note that the approaches and the mediation styles exposed below resemble the research findings of Moser in his study of a rural Taiwanese community.[63]

I am conscious of updating the observations made in this Chapter. In recent years, I have sought to make enquiries from relevant respondents regarding the traditional ideas of non-litigiousness and the use of mediation. In consequence, I have been informed that the cultural tendency to mediate still represents the prevailing norm in Paloh and Tangkak. The traditional attitude of conflict avoidance coupled with the instinctive desire to uphold village harmony continue to be at play. It seems that the essentially non-litigiousness outlook has been preserved. But, of course, with the evolving rural communities in these two places, the village ties are not as strong as before. Commercial relationships have entered the scene and the likelihood of litigation is, comparatively, on the rise. But, what is equally evident is the fact that the *cultural* desire for mediation in the disputing context continues to be perpetuated, despite the fact that modern influences may have largely eroded traditional values in village life.

The Pigs' Case

A villager, Ah Kow, could not speak or understand the Malay language. He was a farmer and he also reared pigs. The pigsty was next to the home of a Malay family. For the Malay family, the Muslim religion considered pigs as ritually unclean animals. It was, therefore, discomforting for the Malay family to live next door to a pigsty.

The Malay house-owner approached Ah Kow to request him to move his pigsty to another part of the farm. Ah Kow could not understand a word of Malay. When he heard the word *babi* (Malay word for 'pig') he innocently called his Malay counterpart *babi*. Naturally, the Malay man lost his temper and beat Ah Kow. Ah

Kow sustained severe injuries. Before he decided to report the matter to the police, he approached Mr Teong Boon Cheow for advice.

Mr Teong listened to Ah Kow's grievance intently and told him that if he wanted the Malay neighbour to be taken by the police for assault he could do so. But, in the circumstances of the case, legal justice was not what Ah Kow wanted. Moreover, Ah Kow harboured the fear that his farm might be secretly destroyed and he would lose his means of livelihood as such.

Since Ah Kow could not speak the Malay language, he invited Mr Teong to be his mediator to discuss terms with the Malay neighbour. Mr Teong obliged. He apologized to the Malay man on behalf of Ah Kow for the unintentional use of the word *babi*, 'fined' the Malay man $30 (as medical expenses for the treatment of the injuries caused to Ah Kow) and requested the Malay man to present Chinese gifts to Ah Kow, i.e. a pair of 'gold flowers' (*bunga emas*) and a piece of red cloth. The Chinese gifts symbolized a return of good luck to Ah Kow's family. Ah Kow later moved his pigsty to the other part of his farm.

In this way, the apparent hostile relations and a lack of mutual trust were cleverly avoided by means of mediation. The formal law could perhaps achieve legal justice, but not social harmony.

The Songster's Case

During the Malayan Emergency, the outskirts of Tangkak were declared 'black' areas due to Communist penetration. The Government subsequently resettled the residents in the new villages in Tangkak. This meant that most people had to start life anew since the re-settlement caused many new settlers to lose their previous jobs.

One Ah Tiam, a Teochew, was very poor and he started earning his living by singing songs in front of houses and shops. Some sympathisers would throw him some money. As this went on day after day, he became a source of nuisance to the householders and the shopkeepers. They started chasing him away and they threatened to hand him to the police.

Although Mr Teong was a Hokkien and at that time, the Hokkien Eng Choon Association Chairman, he was much revered by the Tangkak populace in general. As such, Ah Tiam, a Teochew, came to see Mr Teong for advice. Mr Teong's house was also flooded with shopkeepers and householders who wanted the matter settled as quickly as possible. Mr Teong tendered his advice thus: he told the angry folk that Ah Tiam had come to the new settlement without any financial capital and that he was so poor that the only way for him to start surviving was earning money by entertaining others. There was no doubt that the community at large could report the matter to the police but that was not the best way to solve the matter. So, Mr Teong suggested that he would approach the Teochew Association Chairman and inquire if Ah Tiam could sing at particular hours in the Association House so that the audience would have to pay. That sounded an attractive idea. All those present agreed. Mr Teong mediated on Ah Tiam's behalf with the Teochew Association Chairman who supported the suggestion. The dispute was thus resolved amicably and beneficially to all the parties concerned.

What is important to note here is the 'humanity' factor inherent in the process of dispute settlement. Village harmony was restored.

The Angry Youths' Case

There was a coolie quarrel. The quarrel became heated and turned into a fight. A coolie angrily took out a *parang* (a knife) and slashed another. The victim was sent to the hospital and the offender arrested by the police. Both the victim and the offender were of the Teochew clan.

The Teochew Association held a meeting in the Association Hall. The Teochew Clan Chief invited the Hokkien Eng Choon Association Head to participate in the mediation. This gesture, in fact, reflected Mr Teong's reputation and standing amongst the Tangkak Chinese community. Mr Teong was asked to chair the meeting. The Teochew youths who gathered at the Association Hall were an angry lot. They demanded 'an eye for an eye' and wanted to hurt the offender's family. The situation worsened to such an extent that everyone was talking but no one was listening.

Mr Teong told the assembly that the offender was under police custody and it was pointless to seek personal revenge. He advised the youths to look at the whole situation practically and to channel their 'energy' for positive purposes. He suggested that money donations would be most welcome since the victim was poor and could not afford medical fees. Mr Teong himself started the donation scheme by voluntarily giving RM100. There was uncertainty at first but gradually others began to join in and a substantial sum was collected. The youths were told that their prime concern was medical treatment for the victim first, and not to engage in more fights in the mistaken belief of obtaining justice for the victim.

The offender was later tried in a court, found guilty, and served six months in prison. After he was released, he went to Singapore.

This case illustrates that had Mr Teong not succeeded in the mediation, the youths would have got themselves involved in endless and senseless fights. His mediation also helped the youths to act in a rational, positive and constructive way.

The Relative's Case

Mr Teong's relative came to Tangkak to stay for two days. Since Mr Teong was the Hokkien Eng Choon Association Chairman, he had the right to let his relative stay in the Association House. On the second night, his relative went for a movie and when he returned, he found that his luggage was left outside the room.

The relative naturally came to look for Mr Teong in order to solve the matter, which also involved Mr Teong's 'face' because it meant a lack of respect for him by displacing his relative. Mr Teong immediately went over to see the caretaker of the Association for an explanation. The caretaker remained silent throughout. In a fit of anger, Mr Teong slapped the caretaker once on the cheek.

The next day, the caretaker's family came to see Mr Teong to demand 'justice'. Mr Teong explained how the incident occurred and said that if he was in the wrong, he would offer tea as a sign of apology to the caretaker's family.

Later, it was discovered that a member of the Association had removed the luggage out of some mischief. He apologized to Mr Teong and the latter apologised to the caretaker's family. Since the dispute was not very serious, 'mediating tea' was served as a form of damages. The dispute was amicably settled thus.

The Case of the Jealous Wives

Due to daily contact amongst village folk, social friction was inevitable. Petty quarrels were frequent and some were started out of jealousy.

When the late Madam Tan Sok's husband was in charge of coolie labour in Labis, in the State of Johore, in the 1920s, many families stayed together in the same area to open up new lands for cultivation. There were female workers as well who were employed as servants, cooks, sweepers and so on. The female workers often engaged in talk with the male workers. The wives of these male workers were jealous and they threatened to beat the female workers who grew intimate with their husbands. These jealous wives came to see the late Madam Tan Sok, most of them in tears, to solve the problem. The late Madam Tan Sok would advise parties to live 'like brothers and sisters' in the village. After all, their place of residence was not permanent because as long as there was work to be done, they would stay together but after the work was finished, all the villagers would go their separate ways. She reminded them of the hardship they faced in China and that they should not waste new opportunities in the new land by such petty disputes. What was important was for everybody to live harmoniously together. These wives listened to her advice and became more tolerant. They abandoned the idea of beating the female workers. The late Madam Tan Sok also told them to be reasonable: it was of course expected of their husbands to talk to other people while working. 'A husband is not like a sweet,; she told them, 'he cannot just be swallowed because he happens to be talking to somebody else'. It was, therefore, silly to be jealous, and lose one's rationality.

The Case of Child Abuse

While staying in Paloh, the late Madam Tan Sok's neighbour was fond of abusing his child by beating him without any reason. The child's mother could not stop her husband from abusing the child and she ended up in quarrels with her husband. She approached the late Madam Tan Sok for help. The late Madam Tan Sok then went to the neighbour's house and spoke to the father who happened, at that time, to be beating his child. She told him that it was unreasonable for him to beat his own 'bone and flesh'. If the child needed to be disciplined, he should be caned on the buttocks only but not on any other part of the body. She advised the father that young children were prone to be playful and told him of a Chinese proverb: 'Old people need good health and young people need to play'. The father listened to her advice and from then on stopped abusing his child. Family harmony was restored. The mother was very grateful.[64]

The above cases show that what is significant is not whether one party is in the right or in the wrong, but, rather, what is righteous in the circumstances of the case. Village (or communal) norms prevail over the individual's conception of rights. Moreover, as Newell puts it, 'the object of the dispute was not so much to decide the justice of the case as to obtain village harmony'.[65] The idealized village amity is also more possible where villagers find it important to stay together and lead a relatively stable life.[66] At this juncture, one may recall that the Chinese collectivist-Confucian tradition orientates them to the quest for social harmony and group solidarity, not individual rights.

Another matter worth noting is that the Malay *Penghulu* - a Government appointee to look after village affairs in general - is not often sought after by rural Chinese Malaysians for mediation. One reason is that the Chinese prefer to use their own method of dispute resolution,[67] and another is the ethnic barrier. To the Chinese collectivist, the Malay headman is considered an out-group member. Even if the *Penghulu* is ultimately approached, the disputant himself will not be the one requesting help. More often than not, he would engage another kinsman of some political standing in the village to act on his behalf.[68] In this connection, Mr Wu Tien Hwa, a former *Ketua Mesyuarat* (Head of the Local Council) of Tangkak, stated that the cases he had mediated mostly comprised inter-racial disputes relating to official business. This was because his position was bureaucratic and rural Chinese were likely to keep away from bureaucratic people. The common disputes arising amongst the members of the Tangkak Chinese community were often referred to the clan chiefs and other local Chinese leaders for mediation.

The Implementation Of Common Law Justice: A Dilemma

Quite apart from the fact that rural Chinese Malaysians inherit no propensity to resort to the law and the courts, the phenomenon of dispute settlement may also be attributed to the dilemma they face with the implementation of the Common Law Justice System.

The basic law of Malaysia is the English Common Law, although its application is subject to such modifications as 'the circumstances of the States of Malaysia and their respective inhabitants permit and subject to such qualifications as local circumstances render necessary'.[69] English rules of substantive law and procedural law are widely applied. In this connection, the cross-cultural application of an alien legal system on the Malaysian populace gives rise to several difficulties.

On a comparative basis, Papua New Guinea faces the same problem with regard to the Papua New Guineans vis-a-vis the imposition of the English legal system on them. As pointed out by Mr Michael Somare, a Papua New Guinean Prime Minister:

> Most times that people come before a court they have little or no understanding of the legal principles that are at work. This is not their fault. It is the fault of a legal system that has procedures that vary too much from traditional ways of doing things, and legal rules that do not reflect the situation in which most Papua New Guineans live.[70]

The same may be said of rural Chinese Malaysians, and various other races living in Malaysia.[71] A legal system touches on every aspect of an individual's life, at some time or another. And yet, to be subjected to a legal system which operates quite apart from one's accustomed ways of doing things can be disquieting. It becomes hardly surprising for one to quickly jump to the conclusion that justice is an affair of the rich and for the rich. Thus, such a cross-cultural application of a legal system can be baffling to the recipients.[72]

Culturally, the Common Law Justice System runs counter to the rural Chinese Malaysian beliefs. The English judicial process requires of a judge a verdict rather than a compromise solution.[73] This necessarily excludes the Confucian concept of yielding and compromise. In arriving at a decision, the judge is merely concerned with dealing with the precise legal issues, failing to take into account the complex relations of the litigants. On the other hand, in the mediation process, the mediator assumes a wholistic approach to the dispute in question.[74] Besides, the role of the formal courts is viewed in the light of external agencies. This being the case, the judge's decision cannot properly be regarded as an attempt from within the kinship to arrive at social harmony.[75]

In the Western sense, the individual is a citizen-isolate.[76] But, the Chinese social organization is structured in such a way that the family precedes the importance of an individual. As such, different sets of obligations arise. In the Chinese sense, an infringement of the individual's right equals that of an encroachment of the whole family. The offender has to make redress not only to the victim but to his family as well.

The crucial question of forensic language is very real, particularly where most rural Chinese Malaysians are Mandarin-educated or illiterate. The language of the courts in Malaysia is either the English or Malay language. Both these languages are, at most, second languages to the rural Chinese. As such, the Chinese litigants who cannot understand these two languages are dumbfounded by court proceedings. Although there is a heavy reliance on interpreters in the Malaysian courts, the effect of interpretation in itself constitutes a detour to justice, and may even amount to justice denied through incorrect interpretation. Further, the Chinese come from different dialect groups. The provision of a Chinese interpreter for a party in the court can be meaningless if both of them do not understand each other due to the different dialects spoken respectively by them. As such, the average rural Chinese, when entering a court of law, is confronted by the problems of legal jargon as well as alien languages. In this context, 'justice' is better obtained by informal mediation.

Another setback is legal representation. The complexity of the legal system is such that if a lawyer's services are not invoked, the litigants may feel that they are at a gross disadvantage in conducting their own cases. Legal assistance has become an 'obsession'[77] and the simplest lawsuit 'a professional venture'.[78] The common perception of law by the laymen is that law is enshrouded in mystique. Consequently, the lawyer is viewed as an enigmatic figure. As Stewart McCaulay states, 'in Western culture the lawyer has been regarded with both admiration and suspicion for centuries'.[79] The legal profession is a service profession, but its beneficence has always been seriously questioned. In part, this is attributed to the fact that the legal professionals often isolate themselves from the very people who are vowed to be served with fairness, justice and empathy. For instance, in consumer issues, most lawyers are reluctant to help because such cases are not very lucrative. In this respect, Stewart McCaulay observes that 'even lawyers who look more approachable have techniques for avoiding cases they do not want to take'.[80]

Other problems in the implementation of Common Law Justice may be the ritualized court settings, the undue reliance on procedural rules, heavy costs and so on. To have one's case adjudged in the law court is public display of family shame in the Chinese sense and is strongly discouraged. The Western litigation-based society is definitely contrary to the cultural lifestyle of the Chinese.

Conclusion

Essentially, there are two ways of examining the non-legal minds of rural Chinese Malaysians: the traditional aspect and the Common Law Justice aspect. From the traditional aspect, the ordinary business of life has long been regulated by the different strata of Chinese social organization. As such, the role of the courts in private matters has always been reduced to a minimum. In its place, the dispute settlement process appears to be much availed upon for the adjustment of rights *inter partes*.

There is no doubt that gradually tradition is being eroded away due to the physical distance from China and other disintegrating forces, such as Western education and the heterogeneous Malaysian society.[81] Nevertheless, most rural Chinese still share a common regard for law like their forefathers in traditional China. This is the cultural aspect where change will occur very slowly. The non-litigious attitude accords with the Confucian notion of a harmonious society by conforming to *li*. The Legalist implementation of harsh laws and severe penalties continues to be abhorred.

Moreover, in traditional Chinese belief, the courts have always been regarded as formidable places. This attitude allows for the continued existence of private mediation agencies. Such agencies help to promote social cohesion and reduce inter-personal tension to a considerable extent.

The importance of upholding the prevailing social norms implies little need for official sanctions to maintain social order.[82] Amongst the rural Chinese, public censure and social ostracism represent viable means of social control.[83] This allows little room for the exercise of the official law.

As regards the second aspect relating to the application of the Common Law principles, some obvious handicaps in cross-culturalism can be detected. Justice may ultimately be negated since the Common Law system is too formalized, too complex and imbued with procedural rules which are beyond the comprehension of the lay persons. Litigation based on the Western model is alien to a culture where the formal law has been hardly invoked because it concerned itself chiefly with State rights. And now, although Western education has sufficiently acquainted the average Chinese with the idea of liberalism and individualism, going to court implies certain decided disadvantages. For example, litigation is costly, time-consuming, cumbersome, emotionally stressful, agonizing, and, in some cases, personally embarrassing.

It is quite usual to observe in a court of law that the common law judge exhibits no interest in the background to the dispute and insists on dealing with questions of law which are baffling to the litigants. In contrast, it has been said that Chinese magistrates in the past and the economic court judges of the present day in China have been guided by the principle of *heqing, heli, hefa*[84] in the adjudication of disputes rather than strictly abide by the technical aspects of the law.[85] Chinese-style justice is, therefore, contrasted sharply with the English tradition of a 'zero-sum game' of win-or-lose adjudication.[86] Furthermore, forensic languages are alien to the majority of the Chinese litigants. Rather than be subject to humiliation and ridicule, the Chinese aggrieved party perceives more benefits, wisdom and latitude in the traditional dispute resolution methods.

In brief, the process of traditional dispute settlement can be viewed as a viable means of juridical process. It also enables the courts to be rid of the boredom and burden of adjudicating petty disputes and frivolous cases. In the ultimate analysis, traditional mediation constitutes a way of helping to achieve a peaceful and harmonious society by peaceable means.

NOTES

1   A Chinese proverb.
2   On the proposition that there was no legal profession in traditional China, see Bodde and Morris, *Law In Imperial China*, Harvard University Press, Cambridge (Mass), 1967, at page 4; Phillip M. Chen, *Law and Justice: The Legal System in China 2400 B.C. to 1960 A.D.*, Dunellen Publishing Company, New York/London, 1973, at

page 183; K. S. Latourette, *THE CHINESE, Their History and Culture*, Macmillan Company, New York, 1964, at page 469; Mark Elvin, *Changing Stories in the Chinese World*, Stanford University Press, Stanford, 1997, at page 33; Alison E. W. Conner, 'Legal Education in China: A Look At NanDa' (1986) 7 *Singapore Law Review* 181, at page 182; Kevin Tan Yew Lee, 'Economic Development And The Changing Role of Lawyers – A Comparative Study of Singapore, Japan And The People's Republic of China' (1986) 7 *Singapore Law Review* 68, at page 70. It has also been commented upon that the legal profession in the People's Republic of China is a 'young profession': Lucie Cheng and Arthur Rosett, 'Contract with a Chinese Face: Socially Embedded Factors in the Transformation from Hierarchy to Market, 1978-1989' (1991) 5 *Journal of Chinese Law* 143, at page 203; Stanley B. Lubman and Gregory C. Wajnowski, 'International Commercial Dispute Resolution In China: A Practical Assessment' (1993) 4 *American Review of International Arbitration* 107, at page 121.

3   See, for instance, Michael J. Moser, *Law And Social Change in a Chinese Community: A Case Study from Rural Taiwan*, Oceana Publications Inc., London, 1982; Lester Ross, 'The Changing Profile of Dispute Resolution in Rural China: The Case of Zouping County, Shandong' (1989) 26 *Stanford Journal of International Law* 15.

4   D.G.E. Hall, *A History of South-East Asia*, Macmillan & Co., London, 1955, at page 33, referred to in Gordon Means, *Malaysian Politics*, Hodder & Stoughton, London, 1976, at page 26.

5   Yap Pheng Gek, *Scholar, Banker, Gentleman Soldier*, Times Books International, Singapore, 1982, 'Introduction'.

6   Victor Purcell, *The Chinese In Malaya*, Oxford University Press, Kuala Lumpur, 1978, at page 1.

7   Yap Pheng Gek, note 5 above, 'Introduction'.

8   Gordon Means, note 4 above, at page 26.

9   See J.D. Vaughan, *The Manners and Customs of the Chinese of the Straits Settlements*, Oxford University Press, Kuala Lumpur, 1977, at page 43.

10   Victor Purcell, note 6 above, at page 8; J.D. Vaughan, note 9 above, at page 6. See also Alex Josey, *Lee Kuan Yew: The Struggle For Singaore*, Angus & Robertson, Singapore, 1980, at page 25.

11   Victor Purcell, note 6 above, at pages 194-208. See also Yap Pheng Gek, note 5 above; J.D. Vaughan, note 9 above, at pages 5-8.

12   J.D. Vaughan, note 9 above, at page 6.

13   Victor Purcell, note 6 above, at page 8.

14   Yap Pheng Gek, note 5 above. See Khoo Kay Kim, *The Western Malay States 1850-1873: The Effects of Commercial Development on Malay Politics*, Oxford University Press, Kuala Lumpur, 1975, at pages 51-52.

15 J.D. Vaughan, note 9 above, at pages 6-7.
16 J.D. Vaughan, note 9 above, at pages 6-7; Yap Pheng Gek, note 5 above. See also Syed Hussein Alatas, *The Myth of the Lazy Native*, Frank Cass, London, 1977, at page 85.
17 Victor Purcell, note 6 above, at pages 198-205.
18 GOH Bee Chen, *Negotiating With The Chinese*, Dartmouth Publishing Company Limited, Aldershot/Brookfield, 1996, at pages 47-84.
19 Foreword by J.D. Legge in C. Mary Turnbull, *A Short History of Malaysia, Singapore and Brunei*, Graham Brash, Singapore, 1981.
20 V.R. Burkhardt, *Chinese Creeds and Customs*, South China Morning Post Limited, Hong Kong, 1982, at page 82. See generally Lynn Pan, *Sons of the Yellow Emperor: The Story of the Overseas Chinese*, Mandarin Paperback, London 1990, and Frena Bloomfield, *The Book of Chinese Beliefs: A Journey into the Chinese Inner World*, Ballantine Books, New York, 1983.
21 Yap Pheng Gek, note 5 above.
22 Ray Nyce (Shirle Gordon, ed), *Chinese New Villages In Malaya: A Community Study*, Malaysian Sociological Research Institute, Singapore, 1973, at page 108.
23 V.R. Burkhardt, note 20 above, at pages 1-5.
24 V.R. Burkhardt, note 20 above, at pages 150-152. GOH Bee Chen, note 18 above, at page 61.
25 For instance, in my family, my father continues to observe this practice today.
26 GOH Bee Chen, note 18 above, at page 61.
27 R.F. Johnstone, *Confucianism and Modern China*, Victor Gollancz Limited, London, 1934, at page 54, quoted in Wong Choon San, *A Cycle of Chinese Festivities*, Malaysia Publishing House Limited, Singapore, 1967, at page 119.
28 Rene David and John E.C. Brierley, *Major Legal Systems in the World Today*, Stevens & Sons, London, 1985 (third edition), at page 518.
29 K.S. Latourette, *The Chinese: Their History and Culture*, Macmillan Company, New York, 1964, at pages 568-569.
30 The Khoo family in Malaysia is renowned for this practice. My elder sister's married family continues to practise this custom and her children carry the lineage name as part of their personal names.
31 V.R. Burkhardt, note 20 above, at page 85.
32 *Li Chi Chu-su*, quoted in Chu T'ung-tsu, *Law and Society in Traditional China*, Mouton & Co., Paris/La Haye, 1961, at page 91. See also page 46 in Chapter 3 of this book.
33 V.R. Burkhardt, note 20 above, at page 81.
34 Ray Nyce, note 22 above, at page 35.
35 Wm Theodore de Barry, Wing-tsit Chan and Burton Watson (comp), *Sources of Chinese Tradition*, Volume I, Columbia University

Press, New York, 1960, at page 169; Francis L.K. Hsu, *Americans and Chinese: Passage to Differences*, University of Hawaii Press, Honolulu, 1981 (third edition), at pages 315-316.

[36]   GOH Bee Chen, note 18 above, at page 65.

[37]   V.R. Burkhardt, note 20 above, at page 219.

[38]   Wong Choon San, note 27 above, at page 75.

[39]   GOH Bee Chen, note 18 above, at pages 66-67.

[40]   V.R. Burkhardt, note 20 above, at pages 3 and 36.

[41]   GOH Bee Chen, note 18 above, at page 67.

[42]   Wong Choon San, note 27 above, at page 136; see also V.R. Burkhardt, note 20 above, at page 42.

[43]   V.R. Burkhardt, note 20 above, at page 129.

[44]   J.D. Vaughan, note 9 above, at page 48.

[45]   Wong Choon San, note 27 above, at pages 144-147.

[46]   GOH Bee Chen, note 18 above, at pages 68-69.

[47]   V.R. Burkhardt, note 20 above, at page 75.

[48]   In accordance with Chinese convention, I have retained his name in the usual way. This means that the first name, Wu, is his surname. The same convention for Chinese names will be adopted throughout this Chapter.

[49]   This particular piece of research finding was quoted with approval by Pijaisakdi Horayangkura, 'Cultural Aspects of Conciliation and Arbitration: should there still be a "Centre"', APEC Symposium on Alternative Mechanism for the Settlement of Transnational Commercial Disputes, 27-28 April 1998, Bangkok, in the *Proceedings* published by the Arbitration Office, Thailand, at page 345.

[50]   Goh Bee Leong, the author's younger brother, who is now a practising lawyer in Malaysia.

[51]   See Wong Choon San, note 27 above, at page 172.

[52]   Comment by Mr Tay Cheng Hwa, a retired teacher.

[53]   The quotation is a well-known Chinese proverb.

[54]   The author's late grandmother who was highly conversant in Chinese customs, superstitious beliefs and popular Chinese folklore.

[55]   Comment by Mr Tan Yong Tze, Manager of a co-operative shop in Tangkak.

[56]   See also William H. Newell, *Treacherous River - A Study of Rural Chinese in North Malaya*, University of Malaya Press, Kuala Lumpur, 1962, at page 178.

[57]   Martin C. Yang, *A Chinese Village: Taitou, Shantung Province*, New York, 1945, at pages 165-166, quoted in Jerome A. Cohen, 'Chinese Mediation On The Eve Of Modernization' (1966) 54 *California Law Review* 1201, at page 1220; Kung-Chuan Hsiao, *Compromise In Imperial China*, School of International Studies, University of Washington, Seattle, 1979, at page 58; Stanley Lubman, 'Mao and

Mediation: Politics and Dispute Resolution in Communist China' (1967) 55 *California Law Review* 1284, at page 1298; and referred to in Sybille van der Sprenkel, *Legal Institutions In Manchu China: A Sociological Analysis*, University of London The Athlone Press, London, 1962, at page 101.

58   Chin Kim and Craig M. Lawson, 'The Law of the Subtle Mind: The Traditional Japanese Conception of Law' (1979) 28 *International And Comparative Law Quarterly* 491, at page 502. At page 494, on a comparative basis, it is worth noting these authors' assertion that 'Chinese Confucianism stands out as the single most intellectual influence on traditional Japanese thought'. See also Arthur T. von Mehren, 'Some Reflections on Japanese Law' (1957-58) 71 *Harvard Law Review* 1486, at page 1493: 'The persistence in Japanese Society of forms of dispute resolution other than law is striking'.

59   See also Max Gluckman, *The Judicial Process Among The Barotze of Northern Rhodesia*, Chapter on 'The Background To Litigation', Manchester University Press, Manchester, 1967, at page 49.

60   William H. Newell, note 56 above, at page 185; Kevin Tan Yew Lee, note 2 above, at pages 71-72.

61   The respondent wished to remain anonymous.

62   See Leon Comber, *Chinese Secret Societies In Malaya*, Donald Moore, Singapore, 1959; Leon Comber, *The Traditional Mysteries of Chinese Secret Societies in Malaya*, Eastern University Press Ltd., Singapore, 1961; Victor Purcell, note 6 above, at pages 155-173; Sean O'Callaghan, *The Triads*, W.H. Allen & Co., London, 1981, at pages 53-60; Gordon P. Means, note 4 above, at pages 28-30.

63   See Michael J. Moser, note 3 above, at pages 78-90.

64   Interestingly, a parallel mediation case study involving the same affective approach was recorded by Stanley Lubman in respect of the case mediated by Aunty Wu. See Stanley Lubman, note 57 above, at page 1284.

65   William Newell, note 56 above, at page 179.

66   See A. L. Epstein, *Contention And Dispute:Aspects of Law And Social Control In Melanesia*, Australian National University Press, Canberra, 1974, at page 32.

67   William Newell, note 56 above, at page 179.

68   See Judith Strauch, *Chinese Village Politics in The Malaysian State*, Harvard University Press, Cambridge (Mass), 1981, at page 13.

69   Section 3(1) Proviso of the Civil Law Act 1956 (Revised 1972) (Act 67).

70   Quoted in Bernard Nullu Narokobi, 'Adaptation of Western Law in Papua New Guinea' (1977) 5 *Melanesia Law Journal* at page 69.

71   See Salleh Omar, *Village Politics And Traditional Dispute Resolution Methods*, unpublished Faculty of Law Project Paper 1981/1982, University of Malaya; Gurdial Singh Nijar, *The Position of the*

Unrepresented Accused in the Subordinate Courts in Malaysia, unpublished Faculty of Law Master's Thesis 1979, University of Malaya; Kadir Kassim, 'Alternative Forum for the Settlement of Disputes for the Common Man', paper presented at the 1982 ASEAN Law Association General Assembly in Kuala Lumpur, 25 October 1982. See also J. N. Matson, 'The Conflict of Legal System in the Federation of Malaya and Singapore', (1957) 6 *The International And Comparative Law Quarterly* at pages 243-262.

[72]   See Simon Roberts, *Order And Dispute: An Introduction to Legal Anthropology*, Penguin Books, Harmondsworth, 1979, at pages 12-29. In this connection, see also: R H Hickling, 'The Singapore Law Review Lecture: Breaking Apron Strings' (1987) 8 *Singapore Law Review* 75; Nils Christie, 'Conflicts as Property' (1977) 17 *The British Journal of Criminology* 1.

[73]   Simon Roberts, note 71 above, at pages 20-21.

[74]   A. L. Epstein, note 66 above, at page 7.

[75]   D. M. Emrys Evans, 'Common Law In A Chinese Setting - The Kernel or the Nut?' (1971) 1 *Hong Kong Law Journal*, at pages 21-22.

[76]   A. L. Epstein, note 66 above, at page 36; Guy Powles, 'Court Systems of the South Pacific' in *Pacific Courts And Justice*, published by the Commonwealth Magistrates' Association and the Institute of Pacific Studies, Suva, 1977, at page 5: This article can also be found in (1977) 2 *Malayan Law Journal* at pages xv-xxv.

[77]   Jonathan Caplan, 'Lawyers And Litigants: A Cult Reviewed' in *Disabling Professions*, Marion Boyars, London, 1977, at page 95.

[78]   Jonathan Caplan, note 77 above, at page 101.

[79]   Stewart McCaulay, 'Lawyers And Consumer Protection Laws' (1979) 14 *Law & Society Review*, at page 115.

[80]   Stewart McCaulay, note 79 above, at page 124.

[81]   See Wong Choon San, note 27 above, at pages 176-178; Kadir Kassim, note 71 above, at page 7.

[82]   See Sybille van der Sprenkel, note 57 above, at page 129.

[83]   Yap Pheng Geck, note 5 above, at page 6.

[84]   A Chinese proverb quoted in Chapter 3 above.

[85]   Lucie Cheng and Arthur Rosett, note 2 above, at page 225.

[86]   Simon Roberts, note 72 above, at page 201.

6 Conclusion

Often, litigation is the origin of people's troubles and burdens... One red ink mark in court means a thousand drops of red blood among the people.[1]

In the foregoing Chapters, I have attempted to examine the following themes:

(a) Traditional Chinese mediation and how it contrasts with the Western notion of mediation in the Alternative Dispute Resolution literature found in the West. In particular, cross-cultural connotations do have an impact on the different mediation styles and processes and such an appreciation is, therefore, necessary to avoid misunderstandings; and

(b) The essentially non-legal outlook of traditional Chinese, with specific reference to rural Chinese Malaysians. Such an outlook has been the result of the perpetuation of traditional norms and the availability of extra-legal means of access to justice through the informal dispute settlement process. Rather than a recourse to the formal law and the courts, self-help in most cases has been, and is, principally encouraged. Thus, traditional mediation represents the primary mode of dispute settlement among traditional Chinese.

With regard to the traditional Chinese non-litigious attitude, reference has been made to the Chinese legal tradition to trace the historical origin of such non-litigiousness. An analysis reveals the respective roles assumed by the two principal Schools of thought, namely, Confucianism and Legalism. Confucianism is regarded as the more tenacious of the two.

As witnessed, from ancient times the Legalist School of thought has not been favoured by the Chinese in general. The imposition of harsh rules and severe penalties instilled in the Chinese personal fear and abhorrence for the authority of the law. Consequently, the courts were generally shunned. The introduction of laws was regarded as a regrettable necessity, and indicative of moral decline.

On the other hand, Confucianism steadfastly reigned supreme in traditional Chinese philosophic thought. The Confucian ideals of morality emphasized the value of harmony and the virtue of compromise. In the old days, the Chinese scholars were well-versed in Confucian classics, and the Chinese masses were compelled to attend village gatherings where Confucian learning was imparted. In this way, Confucianism penetrated to all the levels of traditional Chinese society. This also enabled it to become the dominant Chinese philosophy, and to influence the Chinese way of life for many centuries. As has been commented upon, 'the Chinese success with mediation has its origins deeply rooted in the philosophy of Confucius which stresses that social conflict interferes with the natural order of life'.[2]

The traditional Chinese cosmological view has always been the trinity of Heaven, Earth and Humanity. In the traditional view, therefore, social disorder would be reflected in a disturbance of the total cosmic order. It was a view widely held that disputes bore meanings both in the social and natural worlds, and that they were interlinked. As such, disputes were strongly discouraged for fear of attracting heavenly wrath. And, if disputes were inevitable, private mediation represented a more congenial method of resolving them. Litigation was hardly ever resorted to.

In the absence of an inclination towards recourse to the law and its machinery for the administration of private justice, the regulation of human conduct in traditional Chinese society was made possible by various other social factors supportive of group cohesion. The family bond was the strongest. Social sanctions represented effective social control mechanisms. Often, what affected the individual's life was not physical infliction of punishment, but public censure. Shame and ridicule acted as agents of social control. There was ever present a keen desire to preserve one's 'face', and to establish good relations, *ganqing*, with as many people as possible. This served to increase one's *guanxi* network. Cultivating *renqing* (i.e. personal goodwill) and relying on *renqing* was seen to be effective in controlling Chinese social behaviour. The concept of *rang*, or yielding, is concordant with the idea of compromise implicit in mediation. As such, the traditional Chinese social institutions found in the informal leaderships like the clans and guilds interacted with relevant Confucian ideology to produce the favourable means of access to justice via the process of dispute settlement. In this way, justice was often achieved not through formal law, but by informal means.

In rural Malaysia, Confucian ethics continue to play a vital role in the everyday life of the rural Chinese folk. There is also the continued perpetuation of Chinese customary norms and social precepts, in addition to the inculcation of Confucian ethics. All this is made possible by the establishment of the various Mandarin schools in Malaysia, especially found in village communities with a pre-dominantly Chinese population. These schools seek to impart and entrench the Confucian tradition. In another respect, popular Chinese folklore serves as a means of reinforcing the Chinese cultural heritage. Among rural Chinese Malaysians, traditional Chinese values continue to be religiously upheld through the observances of Chinese customary festivities and ritualistic practices.[3] Tradition truly dies hard. It is hardly surprising that rural Chinese Malaysians, being traditionalists by nature, persist in adopting the non-legal outlook of their immigrant forefathers.

As such, the formal law and justice system, to traditional rural Chinese Malaysians, has not been popularly received. Social sanctions seem to have a stronghold because of the closely-knit nature, especially of rural communities, whereby face-to-face relationships are frequent and regular and personal inter-dependence is unavoidable. Anonymity in a village society is the exception rather than the norm. Hence, public opinion compels social compliance and public censure acts as a means of social control. Additionally, among such traditional Chinese folk, the preservation of 'face' and the significance of *ganqing*, *guanxi*, *renqing* and *rang* constitute viable social pressures. In light of this, wherever possible, the Chinese tend to suppress disputes, or conceal them from the public eye. Therefore, the courts come to be regarded as the last corrective agency.

Moreover, traditional Chinese are a relational people who believe in harmony.[4] Religious practices and ancestral worship are ways of expressing their desire to have a harmonious living on earth. Litigation runs counter to harmony.[5] Interestingly, two very recent studies on commercial dispute resolution in modern China reveal the following attitude which is found to be consistent with

Chinese traditional views towards litigation and the formal process of the law:

> The remarkable discomfort of modern Chinese with the assertion and declaration of rights that finds one side to be in the right and the other side in the wrong is observable both in the behaviour of parties and in the reactions of officials in the PRC and elsewhere.[6]

> On one occasion, when one of the authors suggested to a Chinese official that a foreign client would consider bringing suit in a Chinese court, the official's extreme discomfiture manifested itself in stammering, trembling hands and the agitated observation that "a Chinese wouldn't do that!"[7]

It, therefore, appears that the traditional attitude towards law and the formal justice system is generally borne out in contemporary behaviour.[8] This is so despite recent research findings that litigation among the Chinese may be seen to be on the rise. However, it has also been shown that their primary disputing behaviour favours mediation or conciliation as a means of dispute settlement.[9]

It must be recognized that litigation represents the publication of a dispute. Such publicity entails a loss of 'face', the disparagement of *ganqing* and the drainage of financial resources. For example, a Chinese proverb is posited thus: 'Win your lawsuit and lose your money'. The litigant is further potentially made subject to forensic humiliation.

Consequently, the settlement of disputes is a common feature among traditional Chinese, especially in rural areas. Various clan chiefs, family heads and other local leaders have often been called upon to mediate between the disputing parties. The old guilds are superseded by the modern-day chambers of commerce. What is normally expected in such a mediation is the arrival at a compromise solution. When a settlement is amicably reached, the mediation award tends to reflect the relevant aspects of traditional Chinese culture. This means that monetary compensation (considered 'undignified'[10] from traditional times) is rarely sought. Instead, the relief that the aggrieved party is more interested in is the restoration of reputation, both personal and familial. This reiterates the 'face' concept in Chinese culture. As such, the traditional symbolic gifts, for example, red candles, red cloth and gold flowers are more valued than any monetary damages. The serving of Chinese tea as 'mediating tea', in most cases, again reflects the inherent Chinese culture of rites, rituals, respect and hierarchy and, therefore, this form of remedy is seen as appropriate and desirable. Feasting, as we have seen, is used as a normal means to conclude a dispute and signify the success of mediation by restoring inter-group harmony and reparation of ill-will. It, therefore, encompasses both private and public aspects of disputes and their resolution.

However, it must be noted that culture is dynamic and mutable. With the Chinese, some cultural values have resisted the change of time, while others have given way to contemporary pressures. For example, it has been commented upon that the principle of *ganqing* has resisted modern, individualist influence.[11] Erosion of traditional values is made largely true when one takes into account the fragmentation of modern society. As Fukuyama remarks, 'urbanization and geographic mobility weaken lineage organizations'[12] and thus their traditional family values. In communities where human contact is personalized, frequent, and where there is a considerable degree of inter-dependence, as in the rural areas, disputing takes on a different perspective to the one experienced in an essentially urban environment. In the latter situation, strangers care little for the inter-personal associations. There is simply no time for deep socializing. Human values are, therefore, weighed in different terms.

In village communities where the inter-dependent element is gradually vanishing, it has been found that economic ties in the form of contractual relationships have emerged to replace inter-personal bonds. As such, there is a proportionate decline in the reliance on informal dispute settlement techniques.[13] In a study done on the rural Chinese community in Zouping in Shandong, Ross articulated the following observation:

> The increased preference for formal means of dispute resolution arises in part because more is at stake financially in particular contracts. The creation and maintenance of *guanxi* may become less important as impersonal factors grow in importance alongside of and sometimes in place of the personal relationships that otherwise pervade Chinese society. This change is particularly evident in contractual relationships between geographically remote parties where the lack of *guanxi* appears to enhance equality between

parties. It appears that litigation is more likely between parties from different areas than between parties from the same area.[14]

However, despite the above finding, Ross maintains that 'mediation remains the primary dispute resolution medium'.[15]

City folk, by and large, tend to value efficiency, materialism, and pursue personal ends. Their social outlook may resemble closely individualistic values, since mutual dependence is not as strong a factor as in village associations where collectivistic characteristics are featured. Villagers are more inclined towards establishing relationships, and look after communal needs. The effect on conflict management and their respective approaches become apparent. In the case of the city folk, conflicts are personal and not communitarian, and litigation is seen as a normal way of settling individual disputes. Mediation is regarded as a good alternative if it is both economical and expedient. In the case of the villagers, there is a social cost to the conflict. Communal desires for peace, harmony and stability will unconsciously prey upon their minds. Litigation is more likely seen as the last resort. Mediation will be naturally preferred for its concordance with group objectives.

The Chinese who are steeped in their cultural tradition will wish to manage conflicts in amicable ways. But, their immediate environments play a pivotal role in their practical choices in dealing with conflicts. Chinese cultural heritage, as demonstrated in this book, predominantly leans towards the ideal of social harmony, the value of compromise, and the desire for moral as opposed to legal norms. However, a rural Chinese may contrast with an urban Chinese in their respective perception and conception of disputes and their resolution. One factor which accounts for this dichotomy may be that the reduced need for inter-dependence among the urban Chinese disables the flourishing of collectivism.   And, collectivism is a great propeller for mediation. Individualism finds its expression more readily in the urban environment than in the rural environment. As we have seen, individualism promotes justice, pays little regard for social cohesion, and confrontationist behaviour is expected.

Notwithstanding the above observations, by and large, the Chinese do come across ethnologically as a generally non-litigious people. This book attempts to explain why this is so by tracing the Chinese legal tradition and traditional Chinese mediation theory and practice. In ancient days, traditional China was seen as a land of law without lawyers, justice without courts. That was made possible by the prevalence of mediation, which was, in turn, influenced by collectivism, the dominance of Confucianism and necessitated by the fear of the formal judicial system. At this juncture, one may add that tradition persists to the present, and such strong Chinese cultural traits of non-litigiousness coupled with a preference for mediation have endured to this day.[16] As Lubman and Wajnowski similarly point out: 'It is difficult to discern the extent to which traditional and modern ideas have mingled, remain irreconcilable, or coexist....Nonetheless, traditional values continue to manifest themselves today'.[17]

In contemporary China, mediation is still highly regarded and practised on a wide scale, and with strong encouragement of the authorities.[18] Disputes and litigation, seen as a disruption of harmony, are still to be avoided.[19] To echo Lubman and Wajnowski, 'it is striking that PRC official policy since 1949 consistently emphasizes mediation as the preferred method for resolving disputes'.[20] They further observe that:

> 'China's Civil Procedure Law, first enacted provisionally in 1982 and revised and formally enacted in 1991, requires courts to encourage the parties to a dispute to settle matters amicably. Whatever the attention formally given in legislation and policy to litigation in the courts, the Chinese civil legislation that has emerged in recent years is suffused with emphasis on resolving disputes voluntarily by the parties through the assistance of mediators and not by an arbiter of right and wrong, even if such an arbiter – a court or arbitration tribunal – has already accepted jurisdiction over a matter'.[21]

Other commentators such as Folsom and Minan have similarly observed that both the Confucian philosophy and Communist ideology promote 'extensive use of mediation as a method of dispute settlement and social control in modern China'.[22] In the same vein, Palmer asserts that '[t]he value of mediation for society in the present-day PRC is thus viewed in part as a perpetuation of a system of customary ideas and practices that pre-dates socialist rule'.[23]

Elsewhere, the overseas Chinese who have largely inherited traditional Chinese heritage remain mindful of the traditional

Chinese mediation process but as to whether or not its practical implementation is possible will be a question of social setting. As an example, rural Chinese Malaysians who are the adherents of Confucian *li* may be conscious of the traditional Chinese mediation heritage and are still enabled to promote mediation due to the prevailing social sanctions and the existence of village mediators. However, the same picture may not be as true of urban Chinese Malaysians. The latter may feel constrained as the dictates of traditional culture seem displaced by the immediate modern environment. Urban Chinese may not possess sufficient *ganxiwang* (the personal connective network) to enable them to utilize Chinese-style mediation readily.[24] Furthermore, commercial associations may depersonalise the relationships between the parties. Be that as it may, the Chinese, generally speaking, tend towards a non-confrontationist culture due to their inherent desire for achieving social harmony and group goals. As such, mediation will continue and will flourish in the face of modern vicissitudes. As it is, both current trends and past behaviour of the Chinese pre-dominantly indicate the approval of mediation as the accepted first, rather than the alternative, resort to dispute resolution. Consequently, the Chinese are seen to perpetuate their tradition of non-litigiousness.

NOTES

[1]   Wang hui-tsu (1731-1807) in *Tso-chih yao-yen*. *Tso-chih yao yen* is the original Chinese version of *Precepts For Local Administrative Officials* quoted in Sybille van der Sprenkel, *Legal Institutions In Manchu China: A Sociological Analysis*, University of London The Athlone Press, London, 1962, at page 137.

[2]   Ralph H. Folsom and John H. Minan (eds), *Law in the People's Republic of China: Commentary, Readings and Materials*, Martinus Nijhoff Publishers, Dordrecht, 1989, at page 86.

[3]   See Wong Choon San, *A Cycle of Chinese Festivities*, Malaysia Publishing House Ltd., Singapore, 1967.

[4]   See Lucie Cheng and Arthur Rosett, 'Contract With A Chinese Face: Socially Embedded Factors In The Transformation From Hierarchy To Market, 1978-1989' (1991) 5 *Journal of Chinese Law* 143, at page 157.

[5]   Lucie Cheng and Arthur Rosett, note 4 above, at page 221.

[6]   Lucie Cheng and Arthur Rosett, note 4 above, at page 221.

[7]   Stanley B. Lubman and Gregory C. Wajnowski, 'International Commercial Dispute Resolution In China: A Practical Assessment'

(1993) 4 *American Review of International Arbitration* 107, at pages 112-113.

8   Even more interesting is the modern Chinese judicial attitude. Apparently, when judging, the Chinese economic court judges 'believe that their decisions have to go beyond the technical aspect of law, that is not only *hefa*. Their decision must also be congruent to natural reason, *heli*, and appropriate to the feelings of people, *heqing*': Lucie Cheng and Arthur Rosett, note 4 above, at page 225. At footnote no.119 on the same page, the authors further assert that this principle of *heqing, heli, hefa* is the guiding judicial principle upheld by the Chinese magistrates for centuries. It has been noted in Chapter 3 of this book that '*heqing, heli, hefa*' is an old Chinese adage.

9   Stanley B. Lubman and Gregory C. Wajnowski, note 7 above, at page 111.

10   Sybille van der Sprenkel, note 1 above, at page 101.

11   Tahirih V. Lee (ed), *Contract, Guanxi and Dispute Resolution in China*, Garland Publishing Inc., New York and London, 1997, at page xiv.

12   Francis Fukuyama, *Trust: The Social Virtues and the Creation of Prosperity*, The Free Press, New York, 1995, at page 93.

13   See Lester Ross, 'The Changing Profile of Dispute Resolution in Rural China: The Case of Zouping County, Shandong' (1989) 26 *Stanford Journal of International Law* 15, at pages 18-19.

14   Lester Ross, note 13 above, at page 64.

15   Lester Ross, note 13 above, at page 63.

16   Stanley B. Lubman and Gregory C. Wajnowski, note 7 above, at page 111.

17   Stanley B. Lubman and Gregory C. Wajnowski, note 7 above, at page 111.

18   Stanley B. Lubman and Gregory C. Wajnowski, note 7 above, at pages 111-112.

19   Lucie Cheng and Arthur Rosett, note 4 above, at pages 220-221.

20   Stanley B. Lubman and Gregory C. Wajnowski, note 7 above, at page 112.

21   Stanley B. Lubman and Gregory C. Wajnowski, note 7 above, at page 112.

22   Ralph H. Folsom and John H. Minan (eds), note 2 above, at page 86. See also M. Holt Meyer and Charles J. Wysocki, 'Chinese Mediation' (1985) *New York State Bar Journal* 37, at page 38; Jun Ge, 'Mediation, Arbitration and Litigation: Dispute Resolution in the People's Republic of China' (1996) 15 *Pacific Basin Law Journal* 122, at pages 122-125; Michael Palmer, 'The Revival of Mediation in the People's Republic of China: (1) Extra-Judicial Mediation' in W.E. Butler (ed), *Yearbook on Socialist Legal Systems*, Transnational Publishers, Inc., Dobbs Ferry, New York, 1988, at pages 230-231.

[23]   Michael Palmer, note 22 above, at page 231.
[24]   Lester Ross, note 13 above, at page 64.

Bibliography

Alford, W.P. (1995), *To Steal A Book Is An Elegant Offense: Intellectual Property Law In Chinese Civilization*, Stanford University Press, Stanford.

Allocock, Bob (1978), 'The Small Claims Tribunal', *Hong Kong Law Journal*, vol. 8, p.144.

Allcock, Bob (1980), 'Litigants in Person', *Hong Kong Law Journal*, vol. 10, p.257.

Allee, Mark A. (1994), *Law and Local Society In Late Imperial China:Northern Taiwan in the Nineteenth Century*, Stanford University Press, Stanford.

Anderson, E.N. and Anderson, Marja L. (1977), *Fishing In Troubled Waters: Research on The Chinese Fishing Industry In West Malaysia*, The Orient Cultural Service, Taipei.

Arbitration Office of Thailand (1998), *Proceedings* of the APEC Symposium on Alternative Mechanism for the Settlement of Transnational Commercial Disputes, 27-28 April 1998, Bangkok.

Ardagh, A. (1998), 'Lawyers And Mediation: Beyond The Adversarial System?', *Australian Dispute Resolution Journal*, p.72.

ASEAN Law Association General Assembly (1982), *Report*.

Astor, H. and Chinkin, C.M. (1992), *Dispute Resolution In Australia*, Butterworths, Sydney.

Auerbach, J.S. (1983), *Justice Without Law?*, Oxford University Press, New York.

Australian Law Reform Commission (August 1997), *Review of the adversarial system of litigation: Rethinking legal education and training*, Issues paper 21, Canberra.

Australian Law Reform Commission (June 1998), *Review of the adversarial system of litigation: ADR – its role in federal dispute resolution*, Issues paper 25, Canberra.

Australian Law Reform Commission (August 1999), *Review of the federal civil justice system*, Discussion Paper 62, Canberra.

Barkun, Michael (1964-1965), 'Conflict Resolution Through Implicit Mediation', *Journal of Conflict Resolution*, Vols. 8-9, p.121.

Baxi, Upendra (1981), 'Community Participation and the Law', paper presented at the Federation of Malaysian Consumers' Association Seminar on 'Law, Justice and the Malaysian Consumer', Kuala Lumpur.

Bernhardt, Kathryn and Huang, Philip C. C. (ed.) (1994), *Civil Law in Qing and Republican China*, Stanford University Press, Stanford.

Bird, Isabella L. (1982), *THE GOLDEN CHERSONESE And The Way Thither: Travels In Malaya In 1879*, Oxford University Press, Kuala Lumpur.

Bloomfield, F. (1983), *The Book Of Chinese Beliefs*, Ballantine Books, New York.

Bodde, Derk and Morris, Clarence (1967), *Law In Imperial China*, Harvard University Press, Cambridge, Massachusetts.

Bodenheimer, Edgar (1974), *Jurisprudence: The Philosophy And Method Of The Law*, Harvard University Press, Cambridge, Massachusetts.

Bond, M.H. (ed) (1986), *The Psychology Of The Chinese People*, Oxford University Press, Hong Kong.

Boulle, Laurence (1996), *Mediation: Principles, Process, Practice*, Butterworths, Sydney.

Boulle, Laurence (2001) *Mediation: Skills and Techniques*, Butterworths, Sydney.

Caplan, Jonathan (1977), 'Lawyers and Litigants: A Cult Reviewed' in *Disabling Professions*, Marion Boyars, London.

Carlen, Pat (1976), *Magistrates' Justice*, Martin Robertson, London.

Chan, Wing-tsit (trans & comp) (1963), *A Sourcebook in Chinese Philosophy*, Princeton University Press, Princeton.

Chang, Chung-li (1955), *The Chinese Gentry: Studies On Their Role In Nineteenth-Century Chinese Society*, University of Washington Press, Seattle.

Chen, P.M. (1973), *Law And Justice: The Legal System in China 2400 B.C. to 1960 A.D.*, Dunellen Publishing Company, New York.

Cheng, Lucie and Rosett, Arthur (1991), 'Contract With A Chinese Face: Socially Embedded Factors in The Transformation From Hierarchy To Market, 1978-1989', *Journal of Chinese Law*, vol.5, p.143.

Chi, V Hsing, "A Dissertation Upon the Nature of Law", *The China Law Review*, vol.9, p.22.

Chia, Felix (1980), *The Babas*, Times books International, Singapore.

Chin, Kim and Lawson, Craig M. (1979), 'The Law of the Subtle Mind: The Japanese Conception of Law', *International And Comparative Law Quarterly*, vol.28, p.491.

Christie, Nils (1977), 'Conflicts As Property', *The British Journal of Criminology*, vol.17, p.1.

Ch'u, T'ung-tsu (1961), *Law And Society In Traditional China*, Hyperion Press, Westport.

Clarke, D.C. (1991), 'Dispute Resolution In China', *Journal Of Chinese Law*, vol. 5(2), p.245.

Cohen, J.A. (1966), 'Chinese Mediation On The Eve Of Modernization' *California Law Review*, vol. 54, p.1201.

Cohen, J.A. (1988), *Contract Laws of the People's Republic of China*, Longman, Hong Kong.

Cohen, P.A. and Goldman, M. (eds) (1990), *Ideas Across Cultures*, Harvard University Press, Cambridge, Massachusetts.

Comber, Leon F. (1959), *Chinese Secret Societies In Malaya*, Donald Moore, Singapore.

Comber, Leon F. (1961), *The Traditional Mysteries Of Chinese Secret Societies In Malaya*, Eastern University Press Ltd., Singapore.

Comber, Leon F. (1964), *The Strange Cases of Magistrate Pao*, Charles E. Tuttle & Co., Tokyo.

Commonwealth Magistrates' Association and Institute of Pacific Studies (1977), *Pacific Courts And Justice*, Suva.

Commonwealth of Australia (1997), *International Commercial Dispute Resolution Handbook*, Canberra.

Commonwealth of Australia (1997), International Commercial Dispute Resolution Handbook, Canberra.

Condliffe, Peter (1991), *Conflict Management: a practical guide*, TAFE Publications, Melbourne.

Conner, Alison E. W. (1986), 'Legal Education In China: A Look At NanDa', *Singapore Law Review*, vol.7, p.181.

Cooray, L.J.M. (1976), 'The Administration of Justice in Sri Lanka', *Hong Kong Law Journal*, vol.6, p.67.

Cotterell, A. (1988), *China: A Concise Cultural History*, John Murray, London.

Creel, H.G. (1953), *Chinese Thought*, University of Chicago Press, Chicago.

David, R. and Brierley, J.E.C. (1985), *Major Legal Systems in the World Today*, Stevens & Sons, London.

De Barry, W.T. Chan Wing-tsit and Watson, B. (compl) (1960), *Sources of Chinese Tradition – Volume 1*, Columbia University Press, New York.

De Bono, E. (1985), *Conflicts: A Better Way to Resolve Them*, Harrap, London.

De Bono, E. (1993), *Parallel Thinking: From Socratic To De Bono Thinking*, Viking, London.

Du Cann, Richard (1980), *The Art of the Advocate*, Penguin Books, Harmondsworth.

Elvin, M. (1997), *Changing Stories In The Chinese World*, Stanford University Press, Stanford.

Epstein, A.L. (ed) (1974), *contention And Dispute: Aspects of Law and Social Control in Melanesia*, Australian National University Press, Canberra.

Evans, D.M. Emrys (1971), 'Common law In A Chinese Setting – the Kernel or the Nut?', *Hong Kong Law Journal*, vol. 1, p.9.

Fisher, R. and Brown, S. (1989), *Getting Together: Building Relationships As We Negotiate*, Penguin Books, New York.

Fisher, R. and Ury, W. with Bruce Patton (ed) (1981), *Getting To Yes: Negotiating Agreement Without Giving In*, Penguin Books, New York.

Folberg, J. and Taylor, A. (1988), *Mediation: A Comprehensive Guide to Resolving Conflicts Without Litigation*, Jossey-Bass Publishers, San Francisco.

Folsom, R.H. and Minan, J.H. (1989), *Law In The People's Republic Of China: Commentary, Readings and Materials*, Martinus Nijhoff Publishers, Dordrecht.

Fraser, John (1982), *The Chinese: Portrait of a People*, Fontana/Collins, Glasgow.

Fukuyama, Francis (1995), *Trust: The Social Virtues and the Creation of Prosperity*, The Free Press, New York.

Fung, Yu-Lan (1948), *A Short History Of Chinese Philosophy*, The Free Press, New York.

Ge, Jun (1996), 'Mediation, Arbitration And Litigation: Dispute Resolution In The People's Republic Of China', *Pacific Basin Law Journal*, vol.15, p.122.

Gluckman, Max (1967), *The Judicial Process Among The Barotse of Northern Rhodesia*, Manchester University Press, Manchester.

Goh, Bee Chen (1982/83), *The Traditional Chinese Concept of Law, Justice And Dispute Settlement, With Specific Reference To The Rural Chinese Malaysians*, unpublished Faculty of Law Project, University of Malaya, Kuala Lumpur.

Goh, Bee Chen (1996), *Negotiating With The Chinese*, Dartmouth Publishing Company, Aldershot.

Goh, Bee Chen (1997), 'Sino-Western Negotiating Styles', *The Canterbury Law Review*, p.82.

Goh, Bee Chen (1999), 'Culture – The Silent Negotiator', *Australian Dispute Resolution Bulletin*, p.19.

Goodhart, A.L. (1953), *English Law and the Moral Law*, Stevens & Sons Ltd., London.

Goody, J. (1996), *The East In The West*, Cambridge University Press, Cambridge.

Gudykunst, W.B. (1991) (1994 second edition), *Bridging Differences: Effective Intergroup Communication*, Sage Publications, Newbury Park (California).

Gulliver, P.H. (1977), "On Mediators" in Hamnett, Ian (ed), *Social Anthropology and Law*, Academic Press, London et al.

Gulliver, P.H. (1979), *Disputes and Negotiation: A Cross-Cultural Perspective*, Academic Press, San Diego.

Hall, D.L. and Ames, R.T. (1987), *Thinking Through Confucius*, State University of New York Press, Albany.

Hall, Edward T. (1959), *The Silent Language*, Greenwood Press, Westport (Connecticut).

Hall, Edward T. (1966) (Reprint 1990), *The Hidden Dimension*, Anchor Books/Doubleday, New York et al.

Hall, Edward T. (1976) (Reprint 1981), *Beyond Culture*, Anchor Books/Doubleday, New York.

Hall, E.T. and Hall, M.R. (1990), *Understanding Cultural Differences*, Intercultural Press, Inc., Yarmouth (Maine).

Haynes, John M. and Charlesworth, Stephanie (1996), *The Fundamentals of Family Mediation*, The Federation Press, Sydney.

Heng, Aik Luan (1981/1982), *Certain Aspects of Access to Law and the Legal System by the Portuguese-Eurasians in Malacca: A Socio-Legal Study*, unpublished Faculty of Law Project Paper, University of Malaya, Kuala Lumpur.

Hickling, R H (1987), 'The Singapore Law Review Lecture: Breaking Apron Strings', *Singapore Law Review*, vol.8, p.75.

Hofstede, G. (1994), *Cultures and Organizations: Intercultural Cooperation and its Importance for Survival*, Harper Collins Publishers, London.

Hongskrailers, Montri (1997), 'Institutionalized Mediation In Thailand', unpublished doctoral paper, Bond University, Gold Coast.

Hsiao, Kung-Chuan (1979), *Compromise In Imperial China*, School of International Studies, University of Washington, Seattle.

Hsu, Francis L.K. (1953, 1991 third edition), *Americans And Chinese: Passage To Differences*, University of Hawaii Press, Honolulu.

Hsu, Francis L.K. (1981 third edition), *Americans and Chinese: Passage to Differences*, The University Press of Hawaii, Honolulu.

Hu, Chang-tu (1960), *CHINA: its People, its Society, its Culture*, Hraf Press, New Haven.

Huang, Philip C. C. (1996), *Civil Justice in China: Representation and Practice in the Qing*, Stanford University Press, Stanford.

Jamieson, G. (1970), *Chinese Family and Commercial Law*, Vetch and Lee Limited, Hong Kong.

Josey, Alex (1980), *Lee Kuan Yew: The Struggle for Singapore*, Angus & Robertson Publishers, Singapore.

Josey, Alex (1981), *The David Marshall Trials*, Times Books International, Singapore.

Kadir Kassim (1982), 'Alternative Forum for the Settlement of Disputes for the Common Man (in Malaysia)', paper presented at the ASEAN Law Association 1982 General Assembly, Kuala Lumpur.

Kamenka, Eugene and Tay, Alice Erh-Soon (eds) (1979), *Ideas and Ideologies: JUSTICE*, Edward Arnold, London.

Kao, William Timothy, 'The New Way of Approaching The Law', *China Law Review*, vol.1, p.27.

Khoo, Kay Kim (1975), *The Western Malay States 1850-1873: the Effects of Commercial Development on Malay Politics*, Oxford University Press, Kuala Lumpur.

Koller, J.M. (1970) (1985 second edition), *Oriental Philosophies*, Charles Scribner's Sons, New York.

Latourette, K.S. (1964), *The Chinese, Their History And Culture*, MacMillan Co., New York.

Lau, D.C. (Trans) (1979), *Confucius: The Analects*, Penguin Books, London.

Lee, E. (1985), *Commercial Dispute Settlement In China*, Lloyd's of London Press Ltd., London et al.

Lee, Tahirih V. (ed) (1997), *Contract, Guanxi and Dispute Resolution in China*, Garland Publishing, Inc., New York & London.

Lee, Yan Pou (1935), *When I was a boy in China*, George G. Harrap & Co., London.

Leong, Y.K. and Tao, L.K. (1923), *Village and Town Life in China*, George Allen & Unwin Ltd., London.

Little, Reg and Reed, Warren (1989), *The Confucian Renaissance*, The Federation Press, Sydney.

Lloyd, D. (1977), *The Idea of Law*, Penguin Books, Harmondsworth.

Lloyd, Lord of Hampstead (1979), *Introduction to Jurisprudence*, Stevens & Sons, London.

Lobinger, Charles Sumner, 'An Introduction to Chinese Law', *China Law Review*, vol.4, p.121.

Lu, Martin Wu-Chi (1994), 'The Confucian, Taoist And Augustinian Approaches To Truth And Their Contemporary Implications', *Journal of Chinese Philosophy*, vol.21, p.71.

Lubman, Stanley (1967), 'Mao and Mediation: Politics and Dispute Resolution in Communist China', *California Law Review*, vol.55, p.1284.

Lubman, Stanley B. & Wajnowski, Gregory C. (1993), 'International Commercial Dispute Resolution in China: A Practical Assessment', *American Review of International Arbitration*, vol.4, p.107.

MaCaulay, Stewart (1979), 'Lawyers and Consumer Protection Laws', *Law and Society Review*, vol.14, p.115.

MacCormack, Geoffrey (1989), 'Natural Law and Cosmic Harmony in Traditional Chinese Thought', *Ratio Juris*, vol. 2, p254.

MacCormack, Geoffrey (1996), *The Spirit of Traditional Chinese Law*, The University of Georgia Press, Athens & London.

MacKenzie, D.A. (1986, 1992), *China And Japan: Myths And Legends*, Bracken Books, London.

Macneil, Roderick W. (1986), 'Contract Law in China: Law, Practice, and Dispute Resolution', *Stanford Law Review*, vol. 38, p.303.

McAleavy, H. (1963), 'Chinese Law in Hong Kong; the Choice of Sources in Anderson, J.N.D. (ed), *Changing Law in Developing Countries*, George Allen & Unwin Ltd., London.

McNeill, W. and Sedlar, Jean W. (eds) (1960), *Classical China*, Oxford University Press, New York.

Malaysian Chinese Association Reverence For Our Elders Movement Committee (1982), *A Society Based On Reverence*, Kuala Lumpur.

March, Andrew L. (1974), *The Idea of China*, David & Charles, Vancouver.

Matson, J.N. (1957), 'The Conflict of Legal Systems in the Federation of Malaya and Singapore', *The International and Comparative Law Quarterly*, vol.6, p.243.

Means, Gordon P. (1976), *Malaysian Politics*, Hodder & Stoughton, London.

Merry, Sally Engle (1987), 'Book Review: *Disputing Without Culture*', *Harvard Law Review*, vol.100, p.2057.

Meyer, M. Holt & Wysocki, Charles J. (1985), 'Chinese Mediation', *New York State Bar Journal*, p.37.

Mileski, Maureen (1971), 'Courtroom Encounters: An Observation Study of a Lower Criminal Court', *Law And Society Review*, vol.5, p.473.

Miyanaga, Kuniko (1991), *The Creative Edge: Emerging Individualism In Japan*, Transaction Publishers, New Brunswick.

Moore, C.W. (1987), *The Mediation Process: Practical Strategies For Resolving Conflict*, Jossey-Bass Publishers, San Francisco.

Moser, Michael J. (1982), *Law and Social Change In a Chinese Community: A Case Study From Rural Taiwan*, Oceana Publications Inc, London.

Moser, M.J. (1987 second edition), *Foreign Trade, Investment and the Law in the People's republic of China*, Oxford University Press, New York.

Mulholland, J. (1991), *The Language Of Negotiation: A Handbook Of Practical Strategies For Improving Communication*, Routledge, London.

Narokobi, Bernard Mullu (19770, 'Adaptation of Western Law in Papua New Guinea', *Melanesian Law Journal*, vol.5, p.52.

Newell, William H. (1962), *Treacherous River: A study of the Rural Chinese In North Malaya*, University of Malaya Press, Kuala Lumpur.

Nijar, Gurdial Singh (1979), *The Position of the Unrepresented Accused in the Subordinate Courts in Malaysia*, unpublished Faculty of Law Masters' Thesis, University of Malaya, Kuala Lumpur.

Nyce, R. (edited by Shirle Gordon) (1973), *Chinese New Villages in Malaya: a Community Study*, Malaysian Sociological Institute, Singapore.

O'Callaghan, Sean (1981), *The Triads*, W.H. Allen & Co., London.

Orr, Lindsay (August 2000), 'Aspects of Chinese Style Mediation and Western Style Mediation', unpublished LLM paper, Bond University, Gold Coast.

Palmer, Michael (1987), 'The Revival of Mediation in the People's Republic of China: (1) Extra-Judicial Mediation', *Yearbook on Socialist Legal Systems*, New York.

Pan, Lynn (1990), *Sons Of The Yellow Emperor: The Story Of The Overseas Chinese*, Mandarin, London.

Pan, Yigang and Vanhonacker, W.R. (1992), 'Chinese and American Cultures: Value Structure and Family Orientation – An Explorative Study', Euro-Asia Centre Research Series, INSEAD Euro-Asia Centre, Fontainbleau.

Peristiany, J.G. (1967), 'Law' in *The Institutions of Primitive Society*, Basil Blackwell, Oxford.

Powles, C. Guy (1977), 'Court Systems of the South Pacific', *Malayan Law Journal*, vol.2, p.xv.

Pryles, M. (ed) (1997), *Dispute Resolution In Asia*, Kluwer Law International, The Hague.

Purcell, V. (1965), *The Chinese In Southeast Asia*, Oxford University Press, London.

Purcell, V. (1978), *The Chinese In Malaya*, Oxford University Press, Kuala Lumpur.

Rear, John (1972), 'The Chinese Language and the Law', *Hong Kong Law Journal*, vol.2, p.3.

Rendon, Josefina Muniz (2001), 'When You Can't Get Through To Them: Cultural Diversity In Mediation'
http://www.mediate.com/articles/rendon.cfm

Roberts, Simon (1979), *Order And Dispute: An Introduction to Legal Anthropology*, Penguin Books, Harmondsworth.

Ross, Lester (1989), 'The Changing Profile of Dispute Resolution in Rural China: The Case of Zouping County, Shandong', *Stanford Journal of International Law*, vol.26, p.15.

Salacuse, Jeswald W. (1998), 'So, What Is The Deal Anyway? Contracts and Relationships as Negotiating Goals', *Negotiation Journal*, p.5.

Salleh Omar (1981/1982), *Village Politics and Traditional Dispute Resolution*, unpublished Faculty of Law Project Paper, University of Malaya, Kuala Lumpur.

Schwartz, B.I. (1985), *The World of Thought in Ancient China*, Belknap Press of Harvard University Press, Cambridge, Massachusetts.

Scogin, Hugh T. Jr. (1990), 'Between Heaven And Man: Contract And The State In Han Dynasty China', *Southern California Law Review*, vol.63, p.1325.

Scott, P.A. (ed) (1978), *Man and Nature in Southeast Asia*, School of Oriental and African Studies, University of London, London.

Segaller, D. (1980, 1995), *Thai Ways*, Post Books, Bangkok.

Segaller, D. (1982, 1995), *More Thai Ways*, Post Books, Bangkok.

Smith, C.J. (1991), *CHINA; People And Places in the Land of One Billion*, Westview Press, San Francisco & Oxford.

Stewart, E.C. (1972), *American Cultural Patterns: A Cross-Cultural Perspective*, Intercultural Press Inc., Yarmouth, Maine.

Strauch, Judith (1981), *Chinese Village Politics in The Malaysian State*, Harvard University Press, Cambridge, Massachusetts.

Stromholm, S. (1985), *A Short History of Legal Thinking in the West*, Norstedts, Stockholm.

Sulaiman Abdullah (1977/1978), 'Modern Chinese Law Essay', unpublished LLM paper, University of London, London.

Syed Hussein Alatas (1977), *The Myth of the Lazy Native*, Frank Cass, London.

Tan, Poh-Ling (ed) (1997), *Asian Legal Systems: Law, Society And Pluralism In East Asia*, Butterworths, Sydney.

Tan, Yew Lee, Kevin (1986), 'Economic Development And The Changing Role of Lawyers – A Comparative Study of Singapore, Japan And The People's Republic of China', *Singapore Law Review*, vol.7, p.68.

Tay, Alice E-S and Leung, Conita S.C. (1995), *Greater China: Law, Society And Trade*, The Law Book Company Limited, Sydney.

Triandis, Harry C. (1990), 'Cross-Cultural Studies of Individualism and Collectivism' in Berman J.J. (ed), *Nebraska Symposium on Motivtion 1989: Cross-Cultural Perspectives*, University of Nebraska Press, Lincoln and London.

Tu, Ching-I (1987), *Tradition And Creativity: Essays on East Asian Civilization*, Transaction Books, New Brunswick.

Tu, Wei-Ming (1989), *Centrality and Commonality: An Essay on Confucian Religiousness*, State of New York University Press, Albany.

Turnbull, C. Mary (1981), *A Short History of Malaysia, Singapore and Brunei*, Graham Brash, Singapore.

Van der Sprenkel, Sybille (1962), *Legal Institutions in Manchu China: A Sociological Analysis*, University of London The Athlone Press, London.

Vaughan, J.D. (1977), *The Manners and Customs of the Chinese of the Straits Settlements*, Oxford University Press, Kuala Lumpur.

Von Mehren, Arthur T. (1957-1958), 'Some Reflections on Japanese Law', *Harvard Law Review*, vol.71, p.1486.

Wang, Gungwu (1991), *The Chineseness of China: Selected Essays*, Oxford University Press, Hong Kong.

Wang, Gungwu (1992), *Community and Nation: China, Southeast Asia and Australia*, Allen & Unwin, Sydney.

Weldon, Elizabeth and Jehn, Karen A. (1995), 'Conflict Management In US-Chinese Joint Ventures', Working Paper 95-10, Carnegie Bosch Institute, http://cbi.gsia.cmu.edu/

White, Gordon (1994), 'Democratization And Economic Reform in China', *The Australian Journal of Chinese Affairs*, Issue 31, p.73.

Wiebe, Paul D. and Mariappen, S. (1978), *Indian Malaysians: The View From The Plantation*, Manohar, New Delhi.

Wilhelm, R. (1979), *Lectures on the I Ching: Constancy and Change*, Princeton university Press, Princeton.

Wolski, Bobette (1996-1997), 'Culture, Society and Mediation in China and the West', *Commercial Dispute Resolution Journal*, vol. 3, p.97.

Wolski, Bobette (1996-1997), 'Voluntariness and Consensuality: Defining Characteristics of Mediation?', *Australian Bar Review*, vol.15, p.213.

Wong, Choon San (1967), *A Cycle of Chinese Festivities*, Malaysia Publishing House Ltd., Singapore.

Wu, Teh Yao (1979), *Politics East – Politics West*, Pan Pacific Book Distributors, Singapore.

Yan, Yunxiang (1996), *The Flow Of Gifts: Reciprocity And Social Networks In A Chinese Village*, Stanford University Press, Stanford.

Yap, Pheng Geck (1982), *Scholar, Banker, Gentleman Soldier*, Times Books International, Singapore.

Index